THIS BOOK BELONGS TO

_____

A POST HILL PRESS BOOK
ISBN: 978-1-68261-665-9

AMAZING ANIMALS: CREATIVE BRICK BUILDING WITH STEP-BY-STEP IDEAS
© 2018 BY PAUL BACIO, JR. AND SOFIA CHEN
ALL RIGHTS RESERVED

COVER DESIGN AND INTERIOR LAYOUT BY DAN PITTS

POST HILL PRESS
NEW YORK • NASHVILLE
POSTHILLPRESS.COM

Printed in China

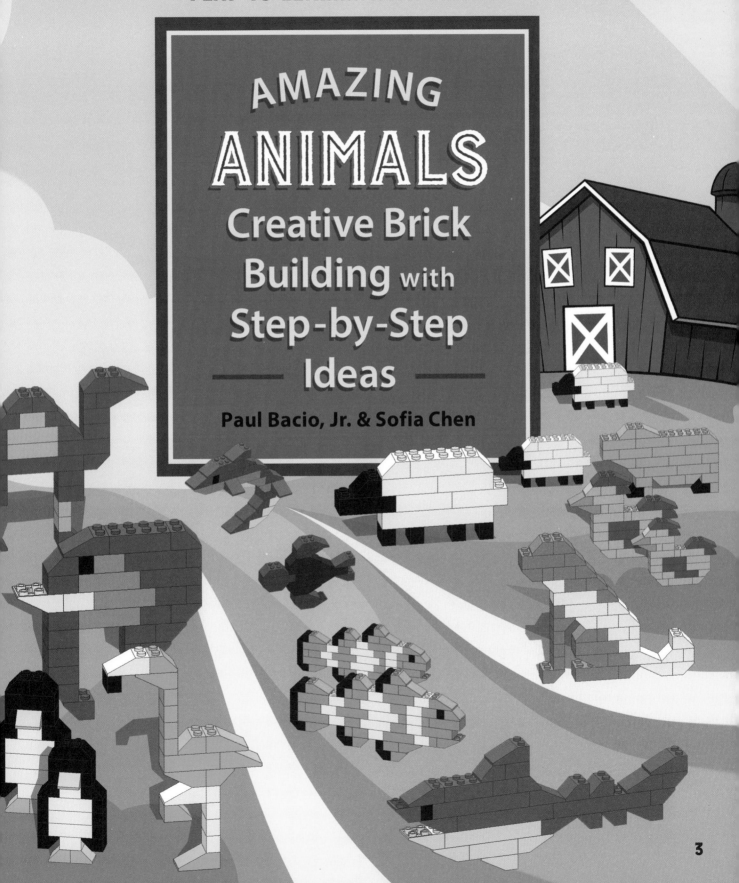

PLAY-TO-LEARN...WITH BRICKS!

AMAZING
ANIMALS
Creative Brick Building with Step-by-Step Ideas

Paul Bacio, Jr. & Sofia Chen

To our
HEAVENLY FATHER,
the Ultimate Creator of all.

For NATALIE,
our Distinctly Special girl.

PRAISE FOR *AMAZING ANIMALS*

"Playing is an essential part of a child's development. This *Play-to-Learn…with Bricks!* series provides creative ways to expose children to a variety of language and pre-academic concepts through a fun and engaging experience."—Kimberly Ng, Speech Language Pathologist

"*Amazing Animals: Creative Brick Building with Step-by-Step Ideas* allows students to actively engage in hands on building with easy to follow step-by-step directions. It is an excellent activity for building fine motor skills while having fun!"—Jenn Mora, Kindergarten Teacher

"I am a parent of two and have been in the early child development field for the past 13 years. After looking over the book I had some of the children in my program use the step-by-step [directions] provided to create various animals. They were all so excited about being able to do them on their own! I loved how the book was so bright and colorful; it absolutely caught their attention. The steps and pictures were so easy for them to understand and follow. As a parent and an educator, I appreciated how the book showed adults all the skills that children are learning while they play with the bricks. I truly believe that children learn best through play and this book is a great example of this!"—Vanessa Sanchez, Preschool Director

"I loved this *Play-to-Learn…with Bricks* series book. I'm a preschool teacher and a mother of two. My daughter (who is 4) loved this book and began building as soon as I gave it to her. She loved the big pictures and all the different animals she could make. I loved the simplicity of the explanations and the big step by step pictures. My daughter was able to build and complete the brick creations on her own, which made her feel so proud of herself. After making a few animals, it got her imagination going to want to build a farm for all her brick farm animals. I highly recommend this book—it is fun, creative, and simple to use."—Yesenia Valdez, Preschool Teacher

"I enjoyed the concepts of this book and felt it was an innovative way of teaching children step-by-step instructions of how to create various objects. The book is user friendly and the colors in them are vibrant. Children enjoy brick building and retain skills through play. So this is a great way for them to learn many cognitive skills, as well as following directions. Having been a preschool teacher for the past 16 years and a mom, I would highly recommend this book."
—Carolyn Tuba, Assistant Preschool Director

"*Amazing Animals* has clear and concise instructions for the kiddos to construct some neat animals. The pages are colorful and the graphics are simple enough for my 3-year-old child to follow along with me. It's not only fun for them to build but they are also [learning to recognize] shapes, colors, and numbers as they go. My kids and I have always had trouble coming up with new ideas of what to build, and usually end up making a building or vehicle. This book has opened our eyes up to a whole new world of possibilities!"
—Erin Rodas, stay-at-home mom of two children ages 8 and 3

TABLE OF CONTENTS

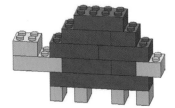

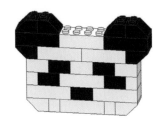

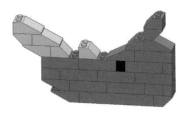

TABLE OF CONTENTS

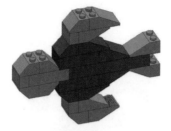

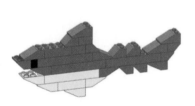

TABLE OF CONTENTS

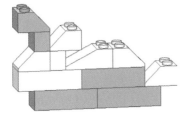

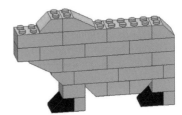

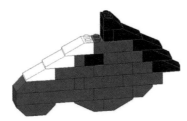
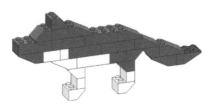

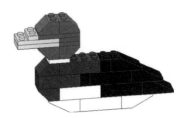

BUILDING BY PICTURES

This brick-building activity book shows you how to build 30 animals. Each activity shows all the bricks that you will need to build your animal. We show the build process in a step-by-step graphic guide and provide Red Arrow indicators that tell you where to put the bricks. This is an activity that you can do with family and friends. Have fun building your animal! Snort-snort! Woof-woof! Quack-quack! Cock-a-doodle-doo!

READY...GET SET...PLAY!

LEVEL INDICATOR

Three levels—EASY, MEDIUM, and ADVANCED—are presented. EASY is for children who are new to brick building. MEDIUM provides more challenging fun with more brick colors integration. ADVANCED involves more complex detailed brick building.

LEARNING CONCEPTS

Each activity has 3 to 4 specific concepts that are provided for parents/caretakers to integrate into their play with the child. Creative play helps with cognitive development. So play, learn, and grow!

THE FINISHED PRODUCT

The picture shows what the completely built animal looks like. You can also get creative and change colors of the bricks...and totally give your animal a unique look! Have fun!

BRICKS - PARTS LIST

All the bricks—colors, shapes, sizes, and quantities—needed to build the animals are listed here for easy reference. Sort the bricks so it will be easier to build later on.

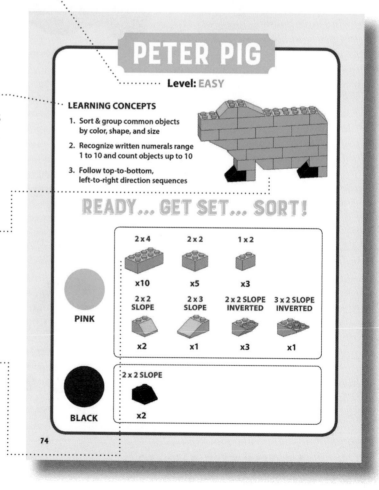

CREATIVE PLAY

The concept of this book is simple. Using the directions provided, parents and care-takers can help their children build different animals out of bricks. These imaginative projects will help your entire family bond as your child has fun and absorbs a number of important developmental concepts. Incorporate learning into playtime as shown in this book—with fantastic results!

These activities will teach your children about the following:

* Recognizing and naming colors
* Familiarity with shapes such as square, rectangle, slopes, and so forth
* Counting objects and counting from 1 to 10
* Recognizing written numerals from 1 to 10
* Simple positioning concepts, such as top, bottom, over, under, beside, and so forth
* Simple directions in sequence (top-to-bottom, left-to-right)
* Sorting and grouping common objects by colors, shapes, and sizes

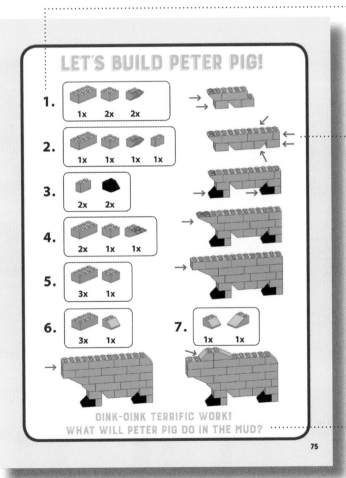

LET'S BUILD PETER PIG!

1. 1x 2x 2x
2. 1x 1x 1x 1x
3. 2x 2x
4. 2x 1x 1x
5. 3x 1x
6. 3x 1x   7. 1x 1x

OINK-OINK TERRIFIC WORK!
WHAT WILL PETER PIG DO IN THE MUD?

75

STEP-BY-STEP

Each step is detailed with the specific bricks that are needed for that step: colors, shapes, sizes, and quantities. This way, it is easier for the child to follow, be prepared, and not get frustrated.

RED ARROWS

The red arrows serve as visual direction cues to guide the child where to place the bricks.

ENCOURAGING WORDS

Words are powerful. Parents and caretakers can make this creative play activity more meaningful with encouraging words that cheer the child on in his/her building endeavor. A child may get stuck with certain steps; when this happens, you can encourage them to try different ways to solve the problem. Be sure to praise the child's effort at the end when he/she completes the animal!

WELCOME TO THE ZOO!

TIMMY TURTLE

Level: EASY

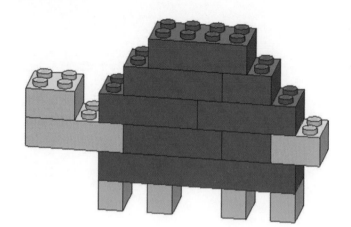

LEARNING CONCEPTS

1. Recognize and name colors

2. Sort & group common objects by color, shape, and size

3. Count numbers, from 1 to 5

READY...GET SET...SORT!

RED

2 x 8	2 x 4	2 x 2
x1	x5	x2

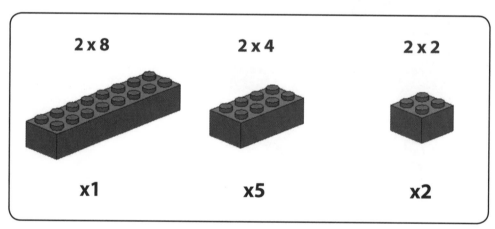

YELLOW

2 x 4	2 x 2	1 x 2
x1	x2	x4

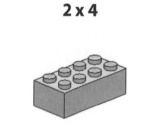

LET'S BUILD TIMMY TURTLE!

1. 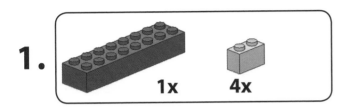   1x   4x   →

2. 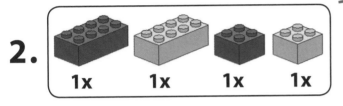   1x   1x   1x   1x   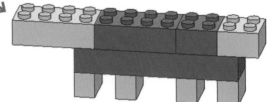

3. 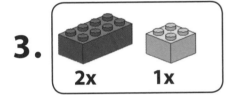   2x   1x   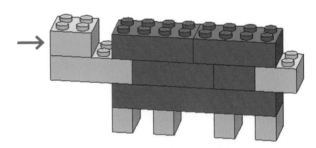

4. 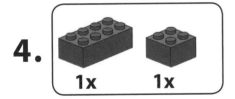   1x   1x   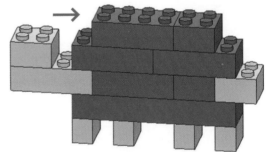

5. 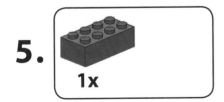   1x   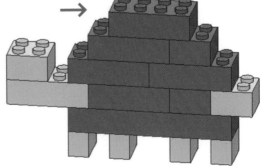

SUPER SHELL! CAN YOU CRAWL SLOWLY LIKE TIMMY TURTLE?

POLLY PANDA

Level: EASY

LEARNING CONCEPTS

1. Recognize and name colors

2. Sort & group common objects by color, shape, and size

3. Count numbers, from 1 to 7

READY...GET SET...SORT!

BLACK

2 x 4	2 x 2	2 x 2 SLOPE	2 x 2 SLOPE INVERTED
x2	x5	x4	x2

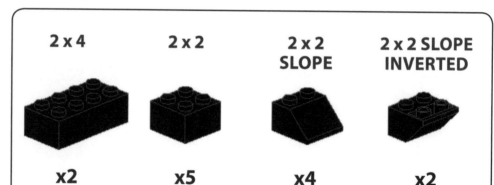

WHITE

2 x 4	2 x 2	1 x 2	2 x 2 SLOPE INVERTED
x7	x3	x4	x2

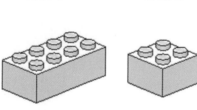

LET'S BUILD POLLY PANDA!

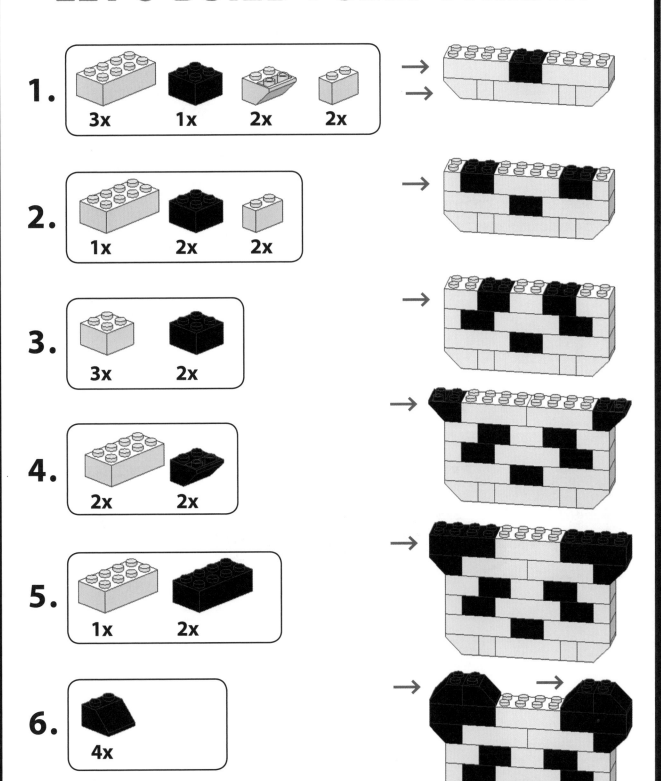

1. 3x 1x 2x 2x

2. 1x 2x 2x

3. 3x 2x

4. 2x 2x

5. 1x 2x

6. 4x

YOU'RE PANDA-PERFECT! WHERE SHOULD
POLLY PANDA LOOK FOR LEAVES?

PENNY PENGUIN

Level: EASY

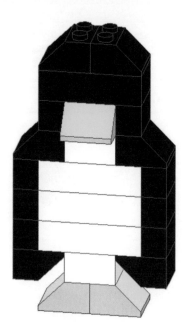

LEARNING CONCEPTS

1. Recognize and name colors

2. Sort & group common objects by color, shape, and size

3. Count numbers, from 1 to 9

READY...GET SET...SORT!

BLACK

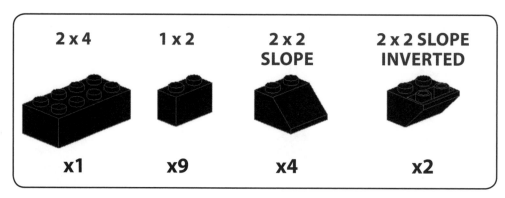

2 x 4	1 x 2	2 x 2 SLOPE	2 x 2 SLOPE INVERTED
x1	x9	x4	x2

WHITE

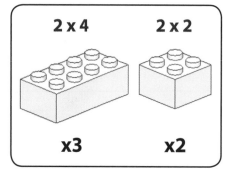

2 x 4	2 x 2
x3	x2

YELLOW

2 x 2 SLOPE

x3

LET'S BUILD PENNY PENGUIN!

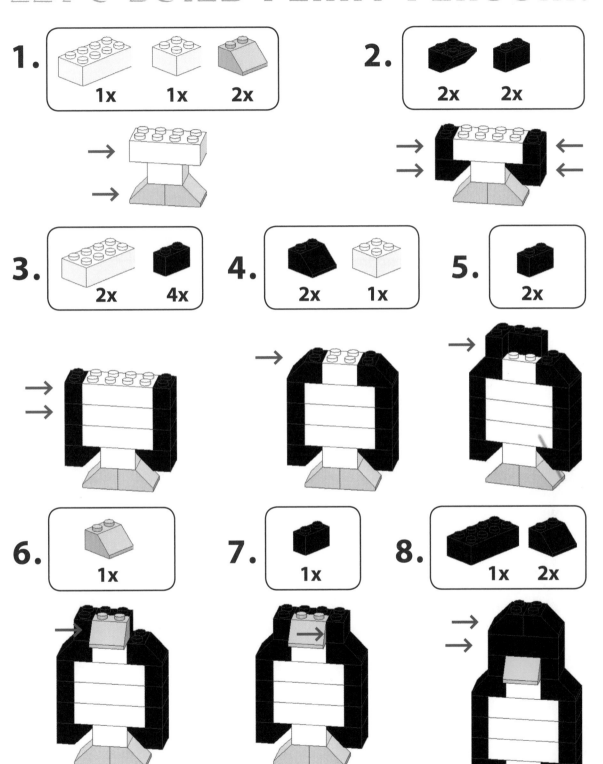

1. 1x 1x 2x

2. 2x 2x

3. 2x 4x

4. 2x 1x

5. 2x

6. 1x

7. 1x

8. 1x 2x

YOU'RE DOING SWIMMINGLY!
LET'S DO A PENNY PENGUIN DANCE!

FREDDIE FOX

Level: EASY

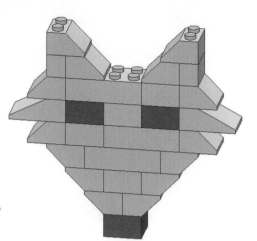

LEARNING CONCEPTS

1. Sort & group common objects by color, shape, and size

2. Recognize written numerals 1 to 8 and count objects up to 8

3. Follow left-to-right direction sequence

READY...GET SET...SORT!

YELLOW

2 x 4	2 x 2	1 x 2

x3	x4	x2
2 x 3 SLOPE	2 x 2 SLOPE	2 x 2 SLOPE INVERTED
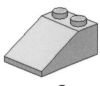		
x2	x8	x6

RED

2 x 2
x3

LET'S BUILD FREDDIE FOX!

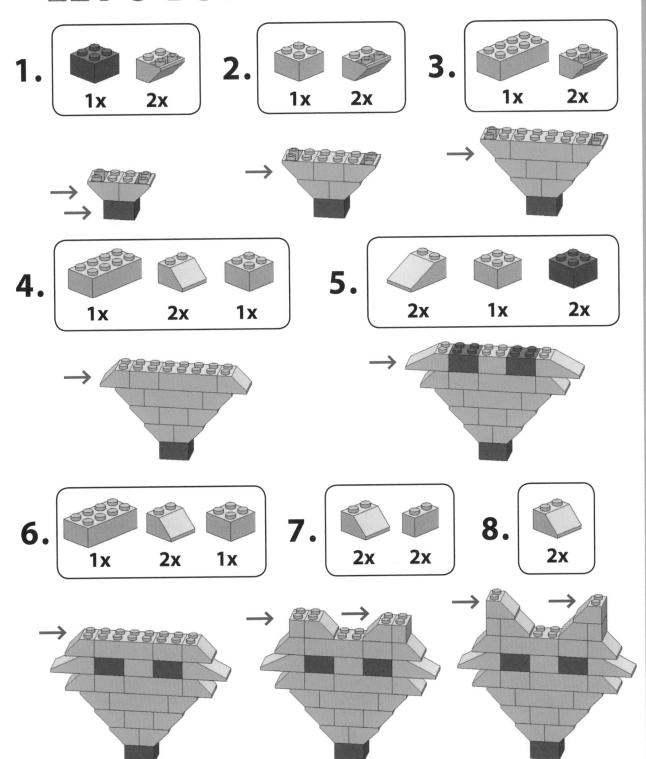

1. 1x 2x

2. 1x 2x

3. 1x 2x

4. 1x 2x 1x

5. 2x 1x 2x

6. 1x 2x 1x

7. 2x 2x

8. 2x

FOX-TASTIC! FREDDIE FOX WANTS TO PLAY.
WHAT SHOULD HE DO?

GIGI GIRAFFE

Level: EASY

LEARNING CONCEPTS

1. Sort & group common objects by color, shape, and size

2. Recognize written numerals 1 to 6 and count objects up to 6

3. Repeat simple patterns

4. Follow left-to-right direction sequence

READY...GET SET...SORT!

YELLOW

2 x 8	2 x 4	2 x 2
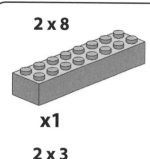		
x1	x6	x3

2 x 3 SLOPE	2 x 2 SLOPE	2 x 2 SLOPE INVERTED	2 x 2 ROUND
x2	x1	x2	x2

RED

2 x 2
x5

BROWN

2 x 2
x2

LET'S BUILD GIGI GIRAFFE!

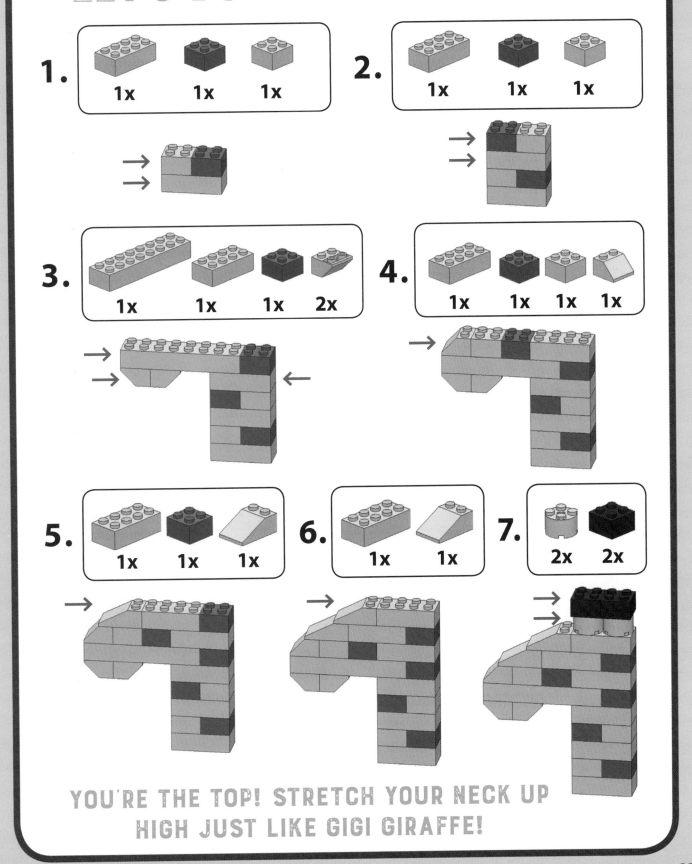

1. 1x 1x 1x

2. 1x 1x 1x

3. 1x 1x 1x 2x

4. 1x 1x 1x 1x

5. 1x 1x 1x

6. 1x 1x

7. 2x 2x

YOU'RE THE TOP! STRETCH YOUR NECK UP
HIGH JUST LIKE GIGI GIRAFFE!

BARRY BEAR

Level: MEDIUM

LEARNING CONCEPTS

1. Sort & group common objects by color, shape, and size

2. Recognize written numerals 1 to 8 and count objects up to 8

3. Follow top-to-bottom direction sequence

READY...GET SET...SORT!

WHITE

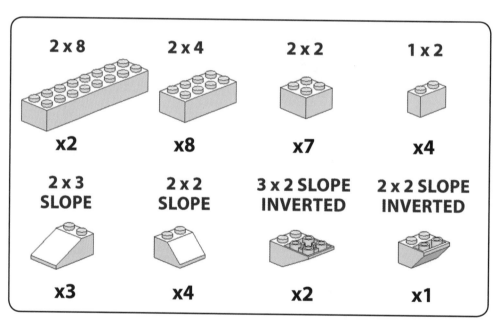

2 x 8	2 x 4	2 x 2	1 x 2
x2	x8	x7	x4

2 x 3 SLOPE	2 x 2 SLOPE	3 x 2 SLOPE INVERTED	2 x 2 SLOPE INVERTED
x3	x4	x2	x1

BLACK

1 x 2	2 x 2 SLOPE
x1	x2

LET'S BUILD BARRY BEAR!

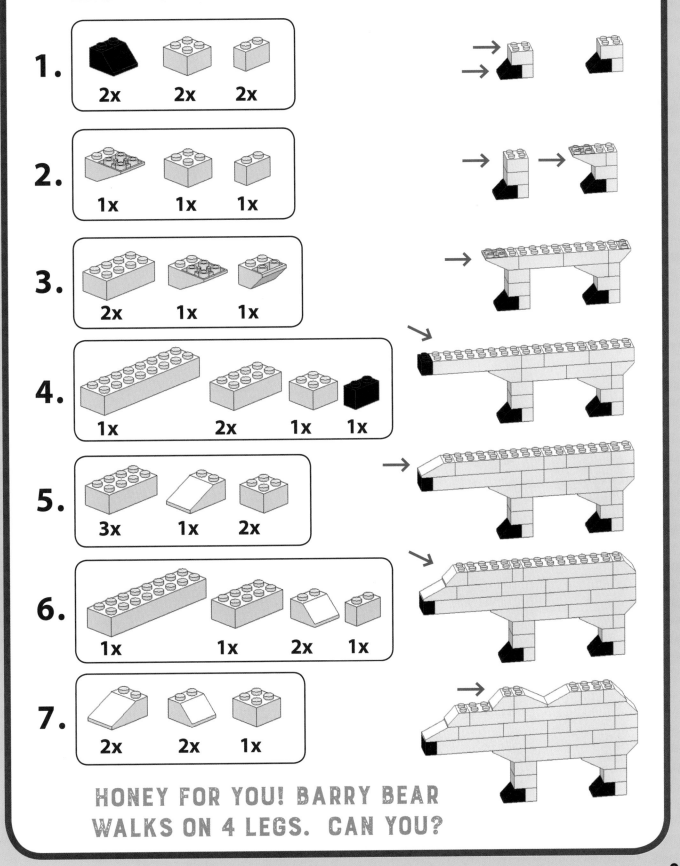

1. 2x 2x 2x

2. 1x 1x 1x

3. 2x 1x 1x

4. 1x 2x 1x 1x

5. 3x 1x 2x

6. 1x 1x 2x 1x

7. 2x 2x 1x

HONEY FOR YOU! BARRY BEAR
WALKS ON 4 LEGS. CAN YOU?

RANDY RHINO

Level: MEDIUM

LEARNING CONCEPTS

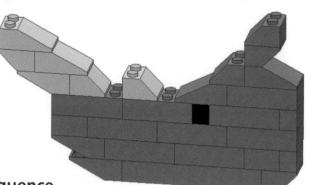

1. Sort & group common objects by color, shape, and size

2. Recognize written numerals 1 to 9 and count objects up to 9

3. Follow top-to-bottom direction sequence

READY...GET SET...SORT!

DARK GREY

2 x 8	2 x 4	2 x 2	1 x 2
x1	x9	x2	x2

2 x 3 SLOPE	2 x 2 SLOPE	3 x 2 SLOPE INVERTED	2 x 2 SLOPE INVERTED
x2	x2	x2	x2

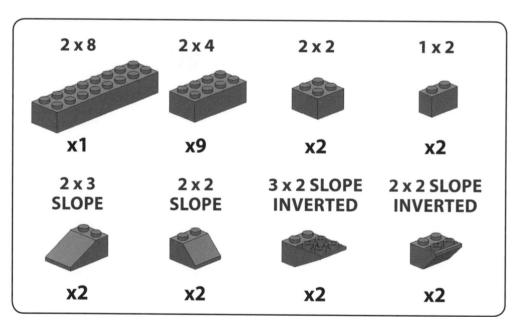

LIGHT GREY

2 x 3 SLOPE	2 x 2 SLOPE	2 x 2 SLOPE INVERTED	3 x 2 SLOPE INVERTED
x2	x2	x1	x1

BLACK

1 x 2
x1

LET'S BUILD RANDY RHINO!

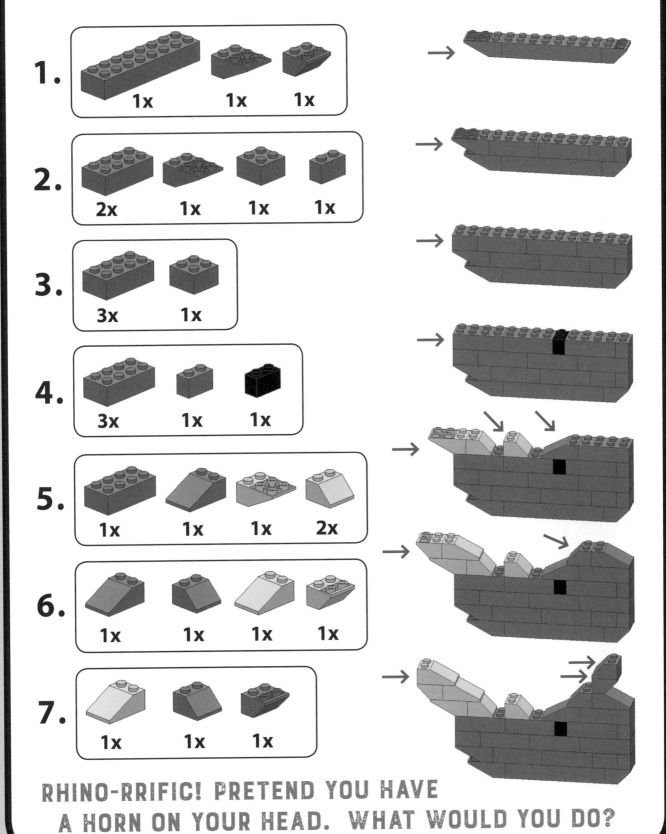

1. 1x 1x 1x

2. 2x 1x 1x 1x

3. 3x 1x

4. 3x 1x 1x

5. 1x 1x 1x 2x

6. 1x 1x 1x 1x

7. 1x 1x 1x

RHINO-RRIFIC! PRETEND YOU HAVE
A HORN ON YOUR HEAD. WHAT WOULD YOU DO?

CAREY CAMEL

Level: MEDIUM

LEARNING CONCEPTS

1. Sort & group common objects by color, shape, and size

2. Recognize written numerals 1 to 9 and count objects up to 9

3. Follow left-to-right direction sequence

READY...GET SET...SORT!

RED

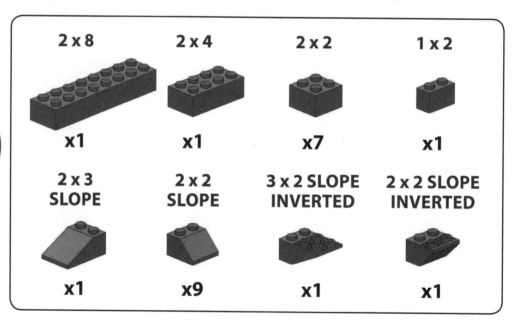

2 x 8	2 x 4	2 x 2	1 x 2
x1	x1	x7	x1

2 x 3 SLOPE	2 x 2 SLOPE	3 x 2 SLOPE INVERTED	2 x 2 SLOPE INVERTED
x1	x9	x1	x1

YELLOW

2 x 4	2 x 2	1 x 2
x2	x1	x4

LET'S BUILD CAREY CAMEL!

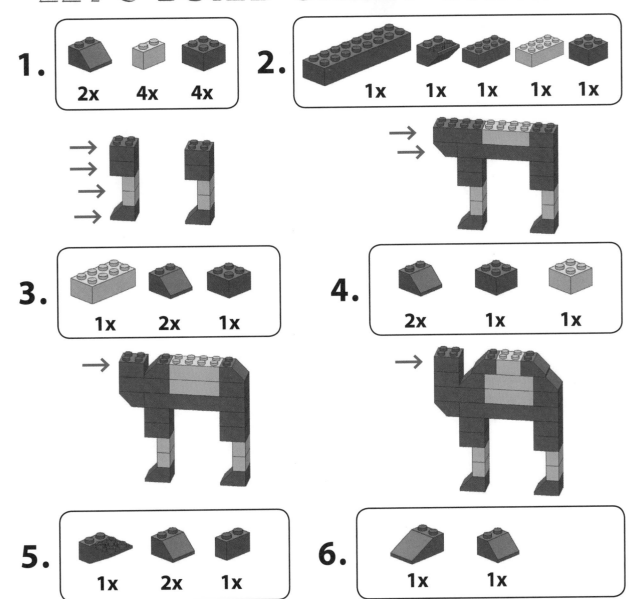

OVER THE HUMP! CAREY CAMEL IS SO THIRSTY. WHERE SHOULD HE LOOK FOR WATER?

EMILE ELEPHANT

Level: MEDIUM

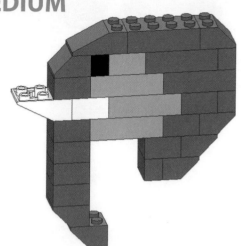

LEARNING CONCEPTS

1. Sort & group common objects by color, shape, and size

2. Understand color gradation concept

3. Follow simple left-to-right direction sequence

READY...GET SET...SORT!

DARK GREY

2 x 4	2 x 2	1 x 2	2 x 3 SLOPE	2 x 2 SLOPE	2 x 2 SLOPE INVERTED
x3	x8	x3	x1	x2	x5

LIGHT GREY

2 x 4	2 x 2
x3	x1

WHITE

2 x 2	3 x 2 SLOPE INVERTED
x1	x1

BLACK

1 x 2
x1

30

LET'S BUILD EMILE ELEPHANT!

1.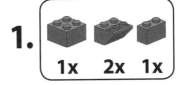
1x   2x   1x

2.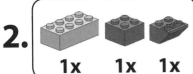
1x   1x   1x

3.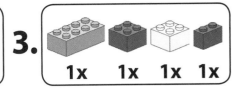
1x   1x   1x   1x

4.
1x   1x

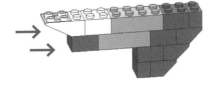

5.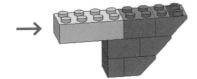
3x   2x

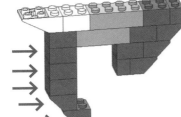

6.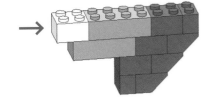
1x   1x   1x

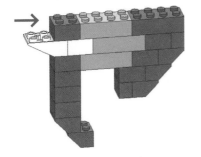

7.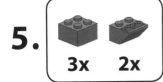
1x   1x   1x   1x   1x

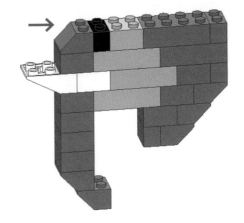

8.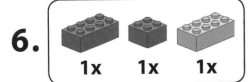
1x   1x   1x

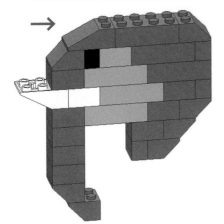

TRUNKS UP! DO AN EMILE ELEPHANT TRUMPET ROAR!

FRANKIE FLAMINGO

Level: MEDIUM

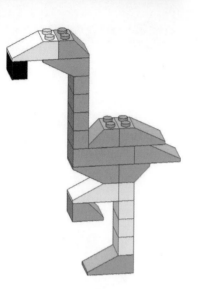

LEARNING CONCEPTS

1. Sort & group common objects by color, shape, and size

2. Understand positioning concept of "above" and "under"

3. Follow left-to-right direction sequence

READY...GET SET...SORT!

PINK

2 x 4

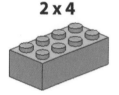

x1

1 x 2

x4

2 x 2 SLOPE

x3

2 x 3 SLOPE

x3

2 x 2 SLOPE INVERTED

x1

3 x 2 SLOPE INVERTED

x2

WHITE

2 x 3 SLOPE

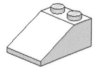

x2

1 x 2

x4

BLACK

1 x 2

x1

LET'S BUILD FRANKIE FLAMINGO!

1.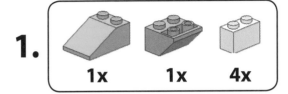

1x 1x 4x

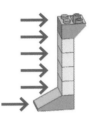

2.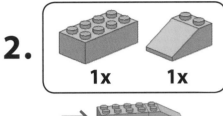

1x 1x

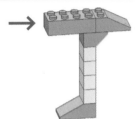

3.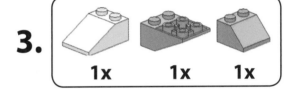

1x 1x 1x

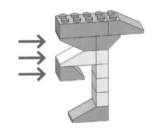

4.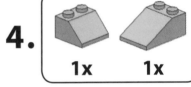

1x 1x

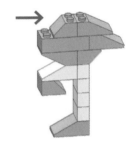

5.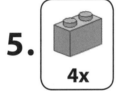

4x

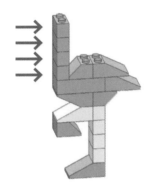

6.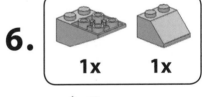

1x 1x

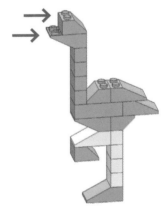

7.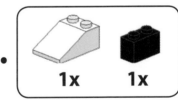

1x 1x

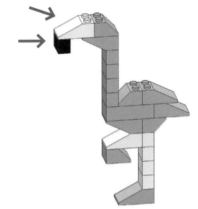

FEATHER
HIGH FIVE!
FRANKIE
FLAMINGO
CAN
BALANCE
ON ONE LEG.
CAN YOU?
YOU TRY!

34

WELCOME TO THE OCEAN!

FRANCIS FISH

Level: EASY

LEARNING CONCEPTS

1. Sort building bricks by color

2. Count which color group has more building bricks

3. Follow directions using the words "top" and "bottom"

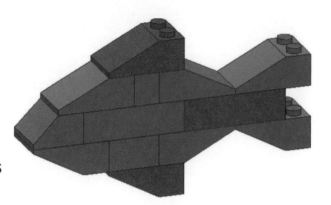

READY...GET SET...SORT!

RED

2 x 4	1 x 2	2 x 2
x1	x1	x1

2 x 3 SLOPE	2 x 2 SLOPE	3 x 2 SLOPE INVERTED
x3	x1	x3

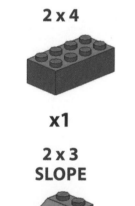

BLUE

2 x 4	2 x 3 SLOPE	3 x 2 SLOPE INVERTED
x1	x1	x1

LET'S BUILD FRANCIS FISH!

1. 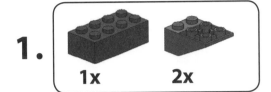 1x   2x

2. 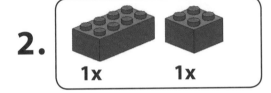 1x   1x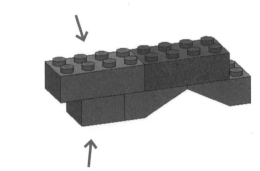

3. 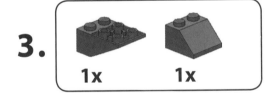 1x   1x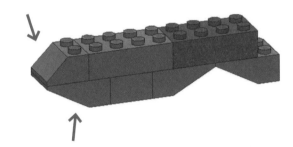

4. 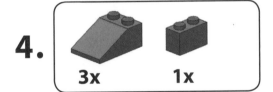 3x   1x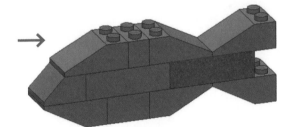

5. 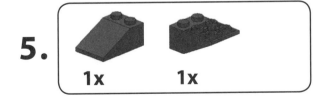 1x   1x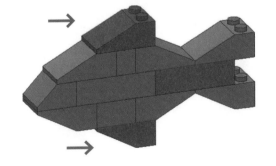

SWISHY JOB! FISH, FISH MAKE A WISH!

SPENCER SEA TURTLE

Level: EASY

LEARNING CONCEPTS

1. Sort building bricks by color

2. Understand the concepts of "big" and "small"

3. Follow directions using the words "top" and "bottom"

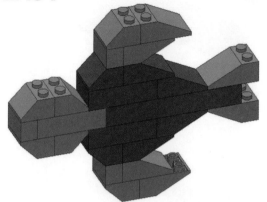

READY...GET SET...SORT!

GREEN

2 x 4	1 x 2	2 x 2 SLOPE
x1	x3	x3
2 x 3 SLOPE	2 x 2 SLOPE INVERTED	3 x 2 SLOPE INVERTED
x3	x3	x3

BROWN

2 x 8	2 x 4	2 x 2 SLOPE

x1	x2	x1
2 x 3 SLOPE	2 x 2 SLOPE INVERTED	3 x 2 SLOPE INVERTED
x2	x1	x2

38

LET'S BUILD SPENCER SEA TURTLE!

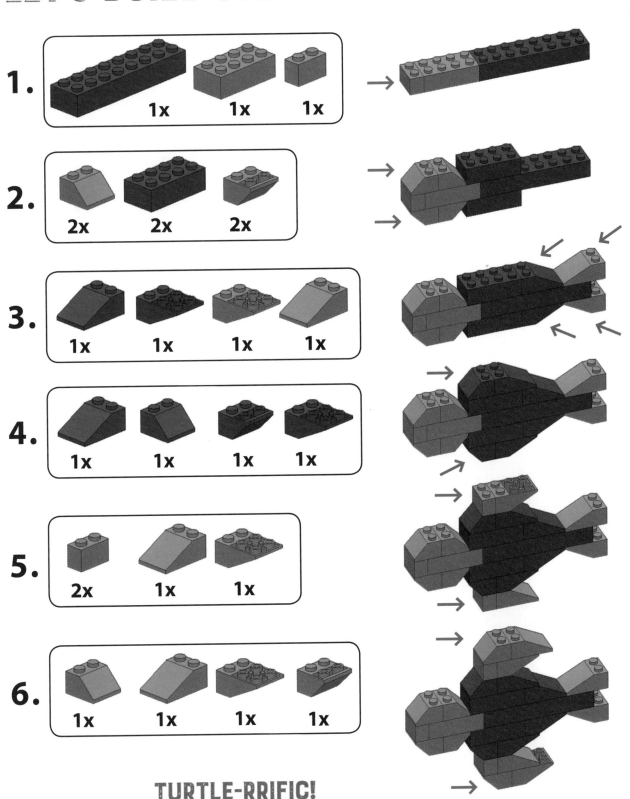

1. 1x 1x 1x

2. 2x 2x 2x

3. 1x 1x 1x 1x

4. 1x 1x 1x 1x

5. 2x 1x 1x

6. 1x 1x 1x 1x

TURTLE-RRIFIC!
TAKE SPENCER SEA TURTLE FOR A SWIM!

SOPHIE STARFISH

Level: **EASY**

LEARNING CONCEPTS

1. Sort building bricks by color

2. Describe color groups using the words "dark" and "light"

3. Follow directions using the words "top," "bottom," and "next to"

READY...GET SET...SORT!

YELLOW

2 x 4	2 x 2	1 x 2
x1	x3	x1

2 x 2 SLOPE	2 x 3 SLOPE	2 x 2 SLOPE INVERTED	3 x 2 SLOPE INVERTED
x2	x1	x3	x1

BLUE

1 x 2	2 x 2 SLOPE	2 x 3 SLOPE	2 x 2 SLOPE INVERTED	3 x 2 SLOPE INVERTED
x1	x3	x1	x3	x1

LET'S BUILD SOPHIE STARFISH!

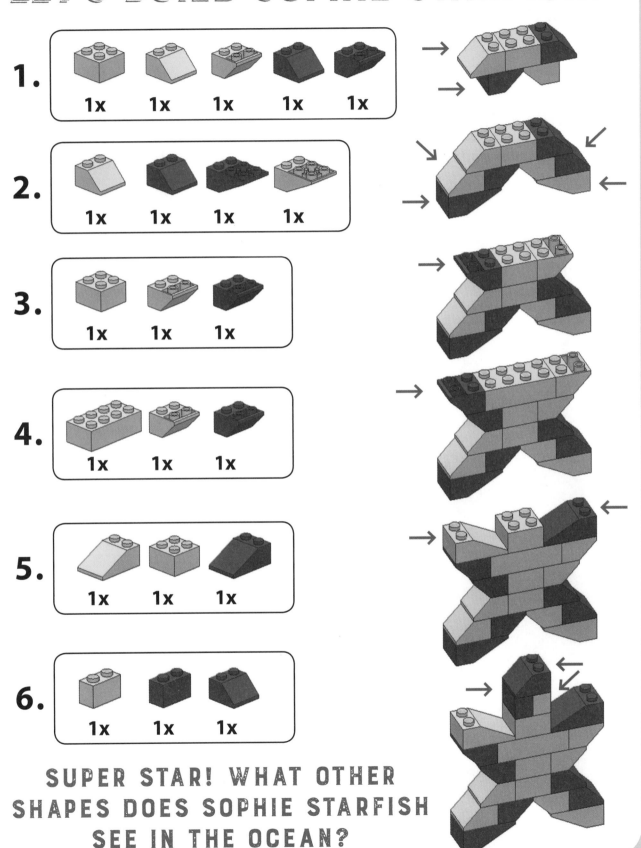

1. 1x 1x 1x 1x 1x

2. 1x 1x 1x 1x

3. 1x 1x 1x

4. 1x 1x 1x

5. 1x 1x 1x

6. 1x 1x 1x

SUPER STAR! WHAT OTHER SHAPES DOES SOPHIE STARFISH SEE IN THE OCEAN?

JOHNNY JELLYFISH

Level: MEDIUM

LEARNING CONCEPTS

1. Make color patterns

2. Stack building bricks and identify which stack is "tall" or "short"

3. Follow directions using the words "first," "second," and "third"

READY...GET SET...SORT!

YELLOW

2 x 8	2 x 2	1 x 2	2 x 2 SLOPE	2 x 3 SLOPE
x1	x3	x4	x4	x2

RED

2 x 2	1 x 2
x2	x4

BLUE

1 x 2

x8

WHITE

1 x 2

x6

LET'S BUILD JOHNNY JELLYFISH!

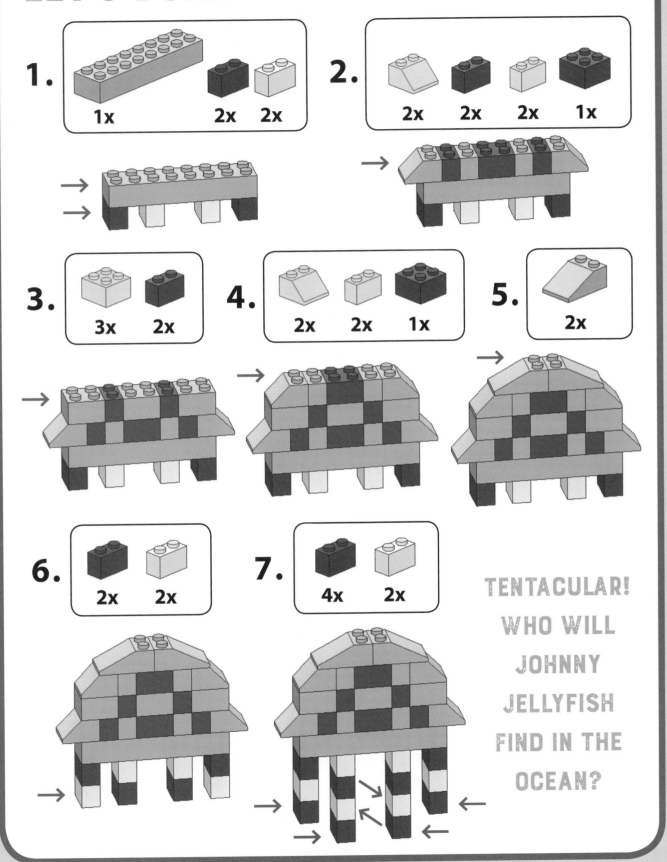

1. 1x 2x 2x

2. 2x 2x 2x 1x

3. 3x 2x

4. 2x 2x 1x

5. 2x

6. 2x 2x

7. 4x 2x

TENTACULAR! WHO WILL JOHNNY JELLYFISH FIND IN THE OCEAN?

DELILAH DOLPHIN

Level: MEDIUM

LEARNING CONCEPTS

1. Make a 3-color pattern sequence

2. Compare building bricks using the words "bigger" and "smaller"

3. Sort & group common objects by color, shape, and size

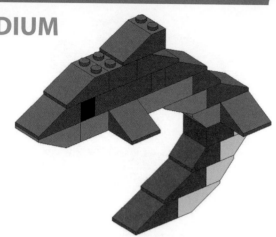

READY...GET SET...SORT!

LIGHT GREY

2 x 4	2 x 2	2 x 2 SLOPE INVERTED	3 x 2 SLOPE INVERTED
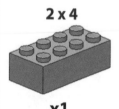			
x1	x1	x1	x2

DARK GREY

2 x 4	2 x 2	1 x 2	2 x 2 SLOPE	2 x 3 SLOPE

x1	x1	x1	x1	x10

BLUE

2 x 2	2 x 2 SLOPE	2 x 3 SLOPE
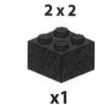		
x1	x1	x2

WHITE

1 x 2	2 x 2 SLOPE INVERTED	3 x 2 SLOPE INVERTED
x1	x2	x1

BLACK

1 x 2
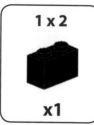
x1

LET'S BUILD DELILAH DOLPHIN!

1. 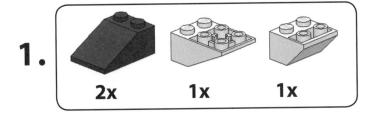 2x   1x   1x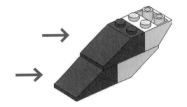

2. 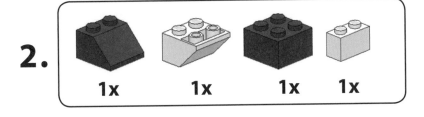 1x   1x   1x   1x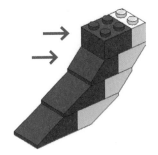

3. 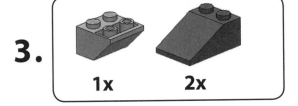 1x   2x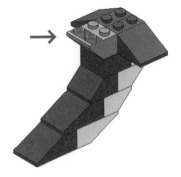

4. 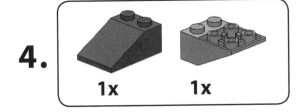 1x   1x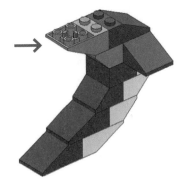

5.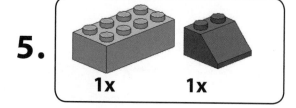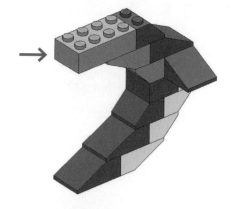

1x   1x

6.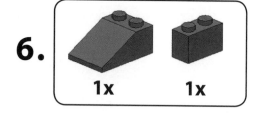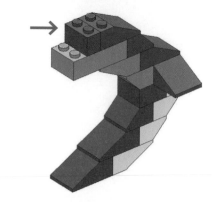

1x   1x

7.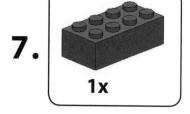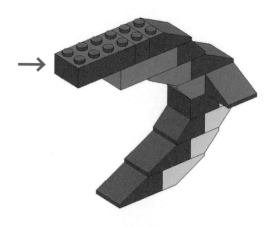

1x

8.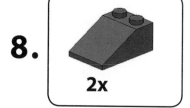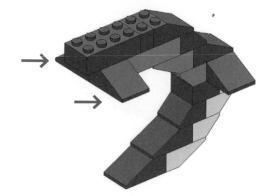

2x

9.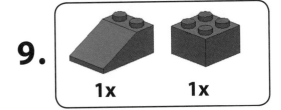

1x   1x

10.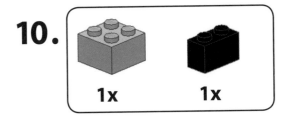

1x   1x

11.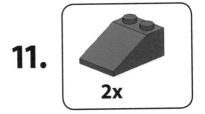

2x

12.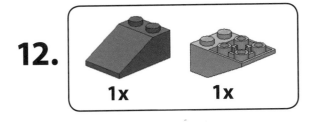

1x   1x

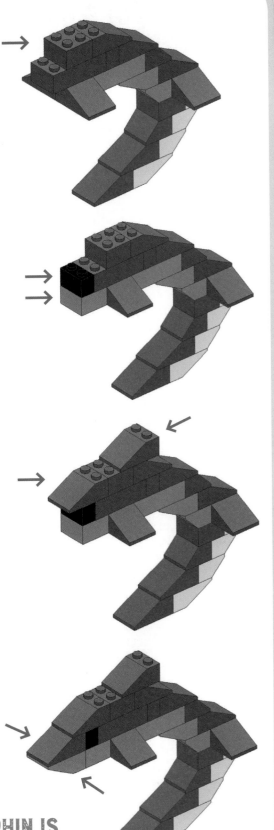

FLIP-FLIP HOORAY! DELILAH DOLPHIN IS
FEELING HUNGRY. WHAT SHOULD SHE EAT?

47

MATTHEW MANTA RAY

Level: MEDIUM

LEARNING CONCEPTS

1. Sort & group common objects by color, shape, and size

2. Find the "smallest" brick and the "biggest" brick

3. Stack 3 different colored bricks and identify "top," "middle," and "bottom"

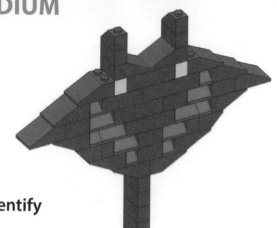

READY...GET SET...SORT!

BLUE

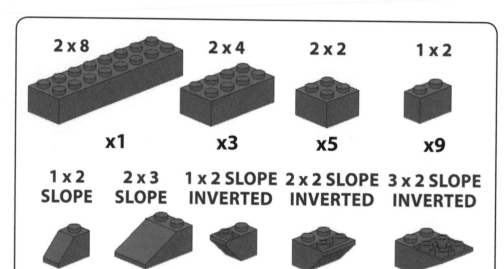

2 x 8	2 x 4	2 x 2	1 x 2
x1	x3	x5	x9

1 x 2 SLOPE	2 x 3 SLOPE	1 x 2 SLOPE INVERTED	2 x 2 SLOPE INVERTED	3 x 2 SLOPE INVERTED
x2	x8	x1	x2	x6

RED

1 x 2 SLOPE	2 x 2 SLOPE
x6	x6

YELLOW

1 x 2 SLOPE
x2

LET'S BUILD MATTHEW MANTA RAY!

1.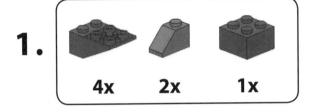

4x   2x   1x

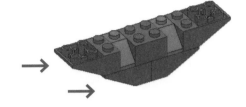

2.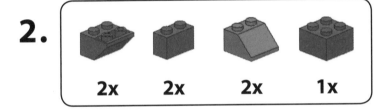

2x   2x   2x   1x

3.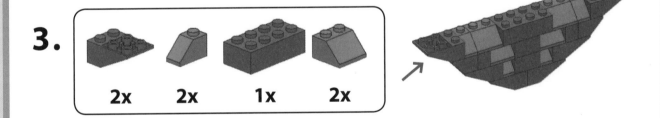

2x   2x   1x   2x

4.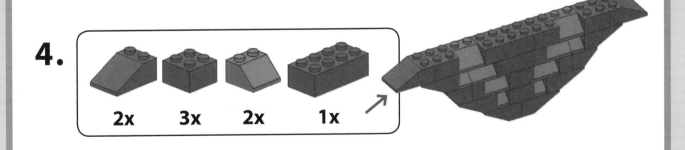

2x   3x   2x   1x

5. 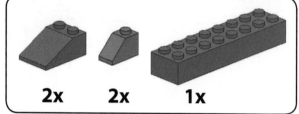 2x 2x 1x

6. 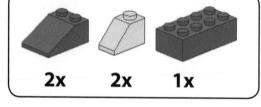 2x 2x 1x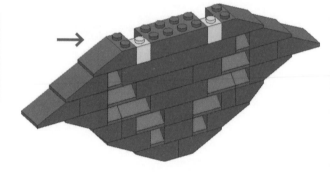

7.  2x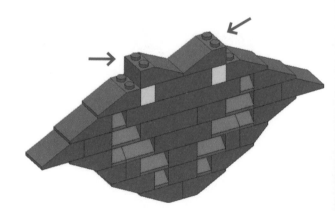

8.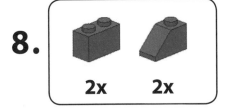

2x   2x

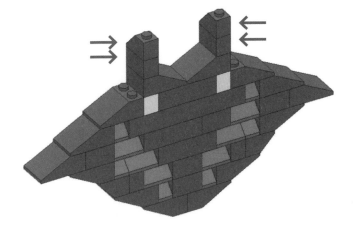

9.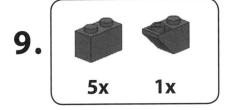

5x   1x

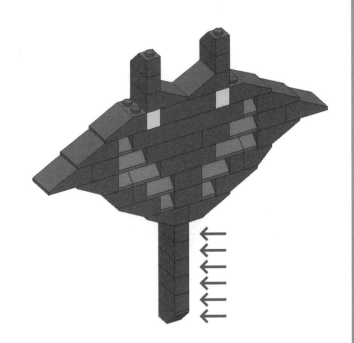

MANTA-NIFICENT! MATTHEW
MANTA RAY IS PLAYING HIDE AND
SEEK. WHERE WILL HE HIDE?

SELENA SHARK

Level: MEDIUM

LEARNING CONCEPTS

1. Sort & group common objects by color, shape, and size

2. Describe each group using comparison words such as "more" and "most"

3. Compare building bricks that are "long" and "short"

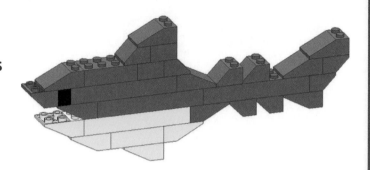

READY...GET SET...SORT!

DARK GREY

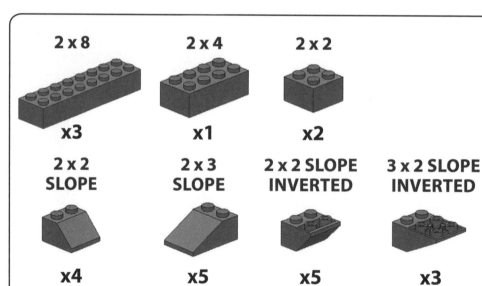

2 x 8	2 x 4	2 x 2
x3	x1	x2

2 x 2 SLOPE	2 x 3 SLOPE	2 x 2 SLOPE INVERTED	3 x 2 SLOPE INVERTED
x4	x5	x5	x3

WHITE

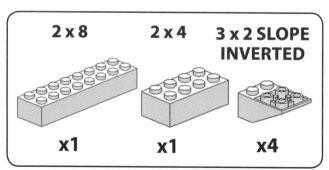

2 x 8	2 x 4	3 x 2 SLOPE INVERTED
x1	x1	x4

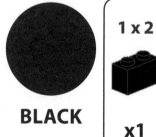

BLACK

1 x 2
x1

LET'S BUILD SELENA SHARK!

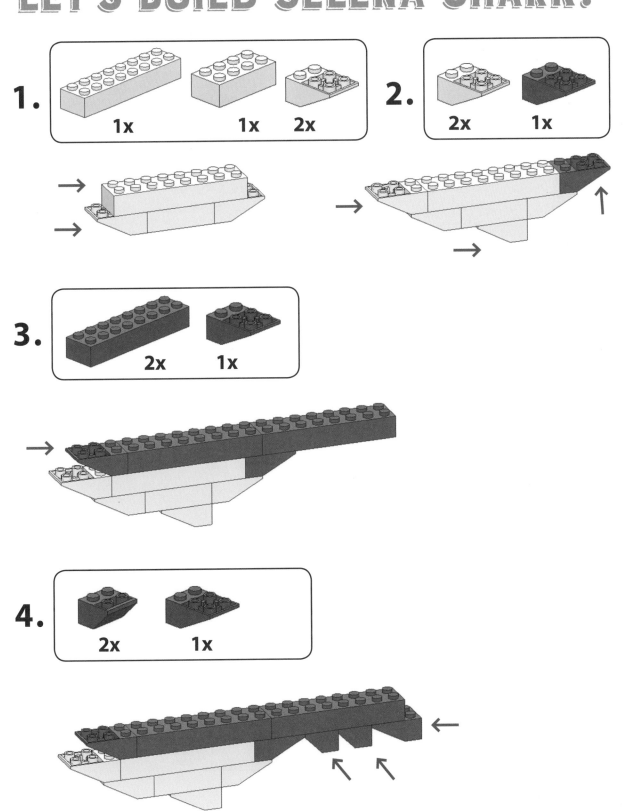

1. 1x   1x   2x

2. 2x   1x

3. 2x   1x

4. 2x   1x

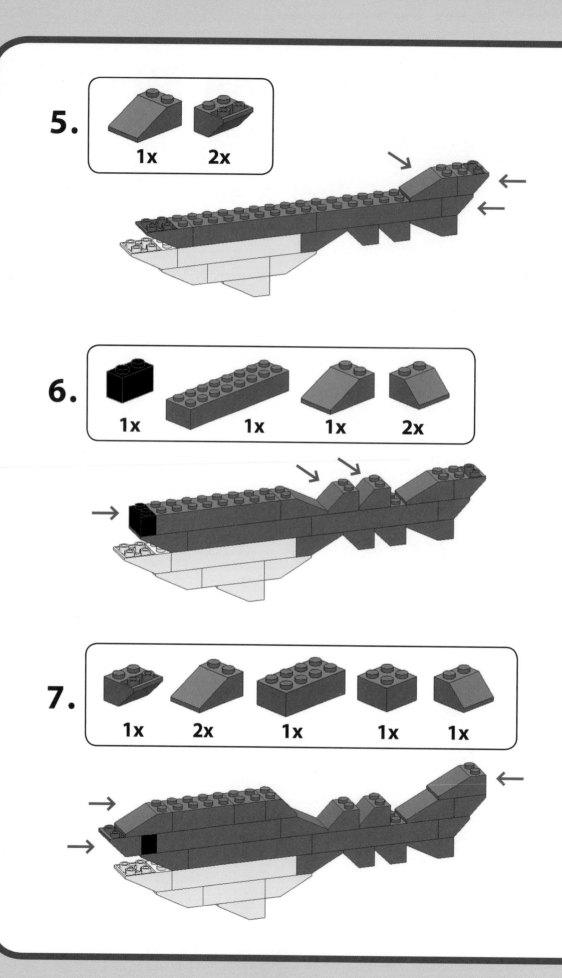

5.

1x 2x

6.

1x 1x 1x 2x

7.

1x 2x 1x 1x 1x

8.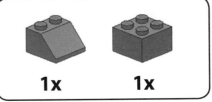

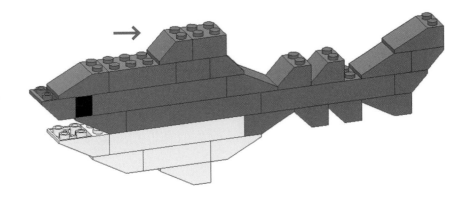

9.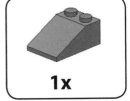

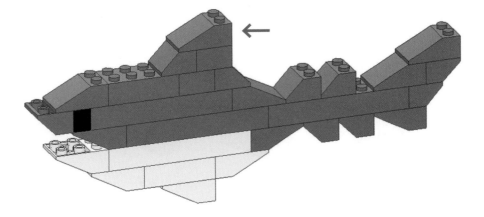

YOU'RE THE TOP SHARK!
HOW DOES SELENA SHARK FEEL?

SAMUEL SEAHORSE

Level: ADVANCED

LEARNING CONCEPTS

1. Sort & group common objects by color, shape, and size

2. Recognize sloping shapes

3. Follow directions using the words "on top" and "under"

READY...GET SET...SORT!

RED

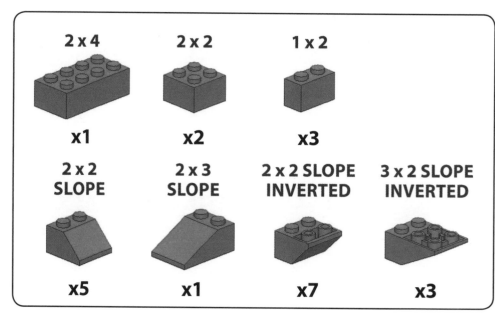

2 x 4	2 x 2	1 x 2
x1	x2	x3

2 x 2 SLOPE	2 x 3 SLOPE	2 x 2 SLOPE INVERTED	3 x 2 SLOPE INVERTED
x5	x1	x7	x3

BLUE

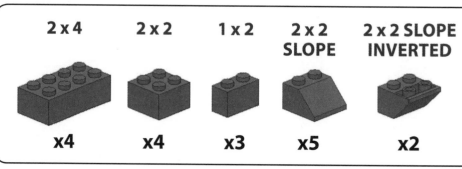

2 x 4	2 x 2	1 x 2	2 x 2 SLOPE	2 x 2 SLOPE INVERTED
x4	x4	x3	x5	x2

LET'S BUILD SAMUEL SEAHORSE!

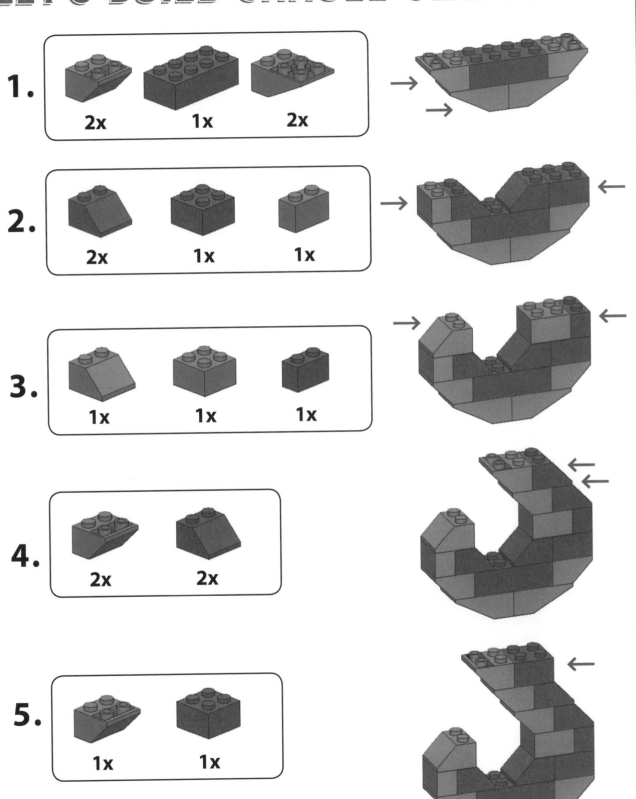

1. 2x   1x   2x

2. 2x   1x   1x

3. 1x   1x   1x

4. 2x   2x

5. 1x   1x

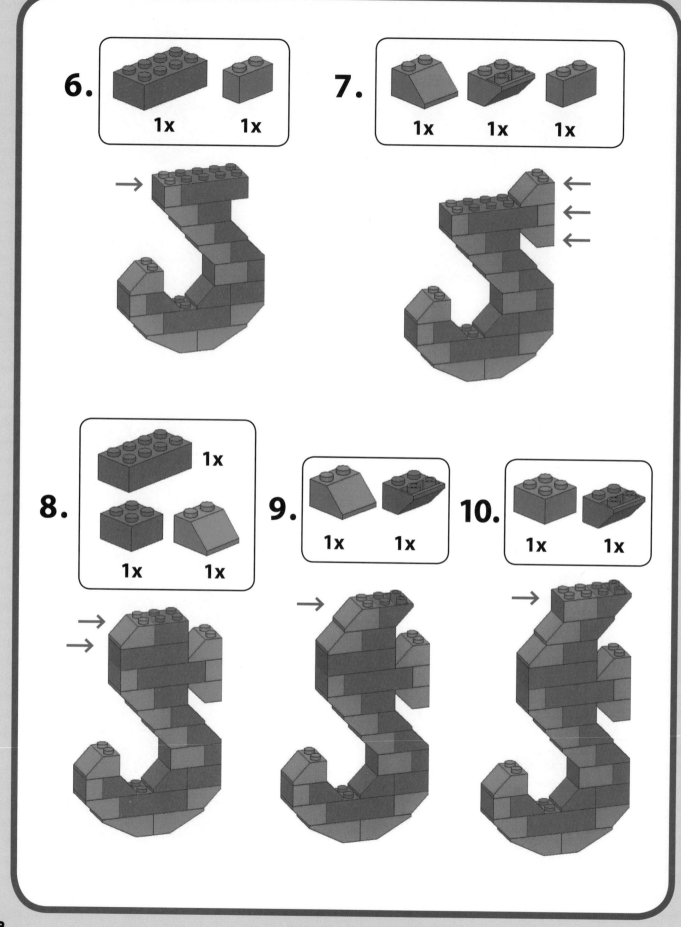

6. 1x 1x

7. 1x 1x 1x

8. 1x 1x 1x

9. 1x 1x

10. 1x 1x

11.

1x 1x 1x

12.

1x 1x 1x

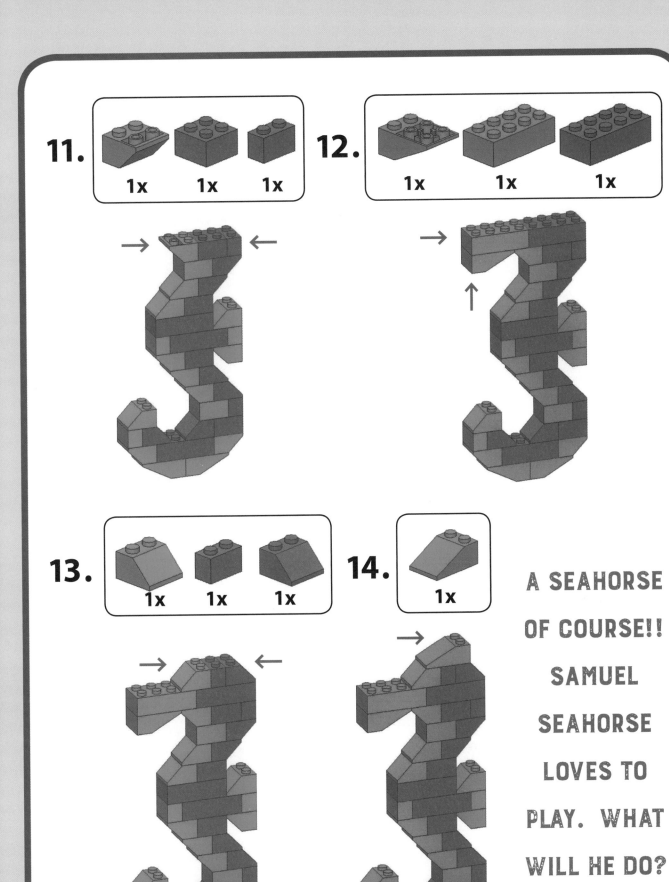

13.

1x 1x 1x

14.

1x

A SEAHORSE
OF COURSE!!
SAMUEL
SEAHORSE
LOVES TO
PLAY. WHAT
WILL HE DO?

CAMILLE CRAB

Level: ADVANCED

LEARNING CONCEPTS

1. Sort & group common objects by color, shape, and size

2. Understand the concepts of "more" and "most"

3. Follow directions using the words "on top" and "under"

READY...GET SET...SORT!

RED

2 x 8	2 x 4	2 x 2	1 x 2
x2	x1	x3	x4

2 x 2 SLOPE	2 x 3 SLOPE	3 x 2 SLOPE INVERTED
x1	x2	x4

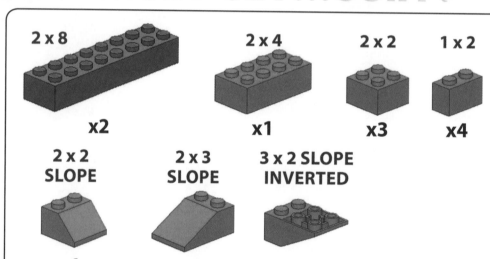

BLUE

2 x 2 SLOPE	2 x 3 SLOPE	2 x 2 SLOPE INVERTED	3 x 2 SLOPE INVERTED
x6	x6	x6	x6

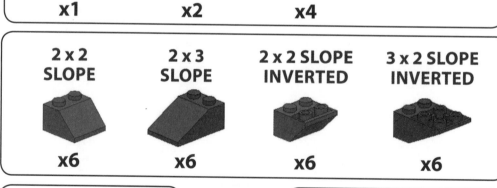

YELLOW

1 x 2	2 x 2 SLOPE
x6	x2

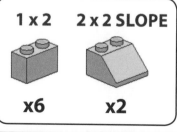

BLACK

1 x 2 SLOPE	2 x 3 SLOPE
x2	x2

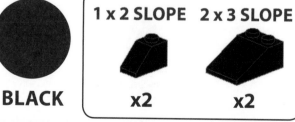

60

LET'S BUILD CAMILLE CRAB!

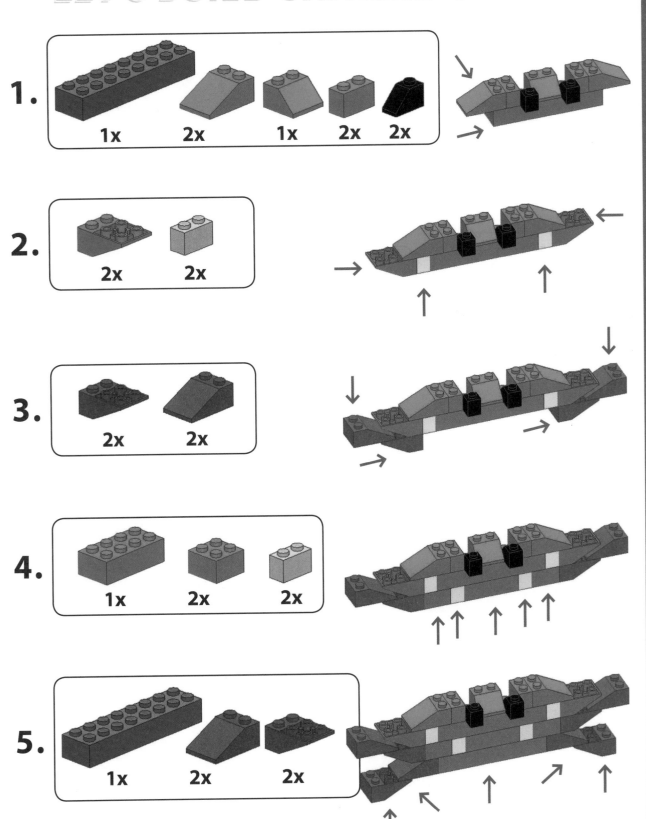

1. 1x 2x 1x 2x 2x

2. 2x 2x

3. 2x 2x

4. 1x 2x 2x

5. 1x 2x 2x

6.

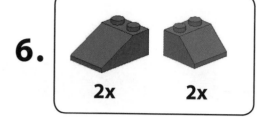 2x 2x

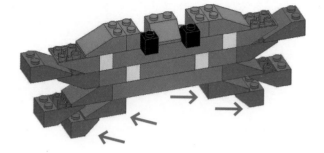

7.

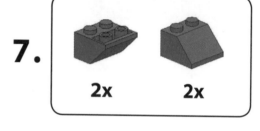 2x 2x

8.

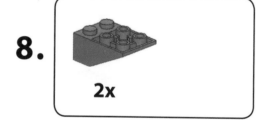 2x

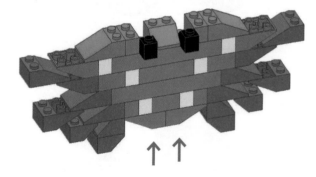

9.

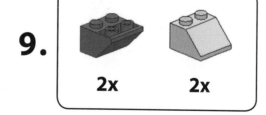 2x 2x

10.

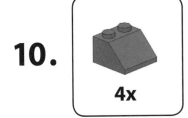

4x

11.

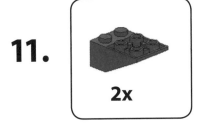

2x

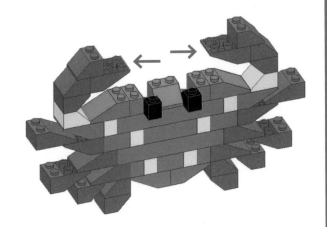

12.

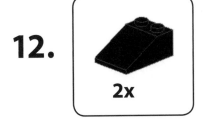

2x

CRAB-TASTIC! CAMILLE CRAB IS LOOKING
FOR TREASURES. WHAT WILL SHE FIND?

CLEMENTINE CLOWNFISH

Level: ADVANCED

LEARNING CONCEPTS

1. Use the words "same" and "different" to sort by color

2. Identify and name colors

3. Follow directions using the words "first" and "then"

READY...GET SET...SORT!

ORANGE

2 x 4	2 x 2	1 x 2
x7	x10	x6

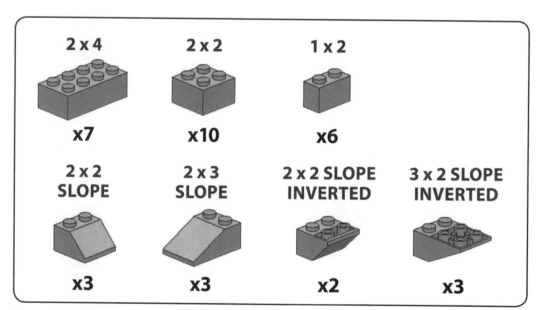

2 x 2 SLOPE	2 x 3 SLOPE	2 x 2 SLOPE INVERTED	3 x 2 SLOPE INVERTED
x3	x3	x2	x3

WHITE

2 x 4	2 x 2
x3	x10

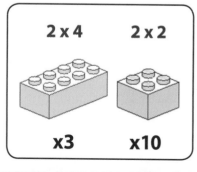

BLACK

1 x 2	2 x 2 SLOPE	2 x 2 SLOPE INVERTED
x8	x3	x3

LET'S BUILD CLEMENTINE CLOWNFISH!

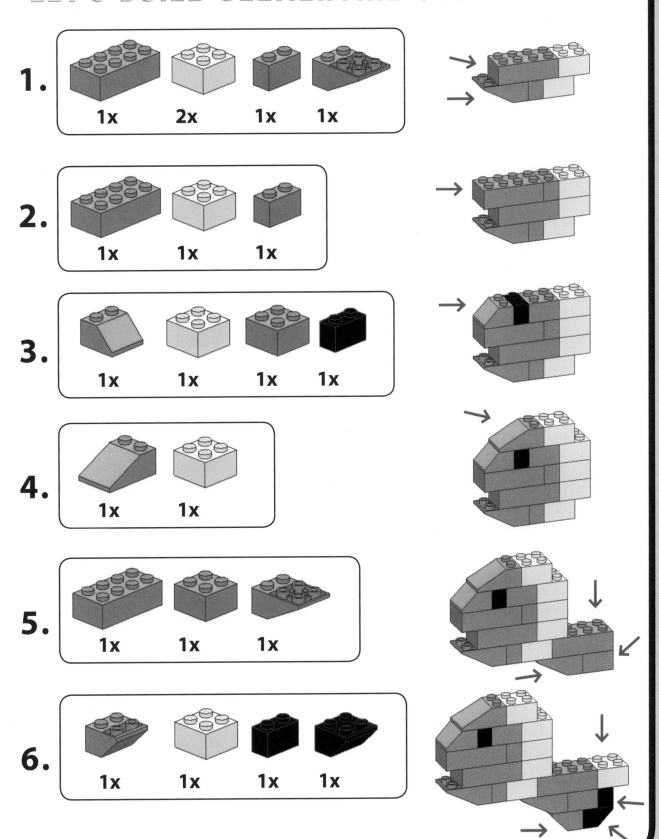

1. 1x 2x 1x 1x

2. 1x 1x 1x

3. 1x 1x 1x 1x

4. 1x 1x

5. 1x 1x 1x

6. 1x 1x 1x 1x

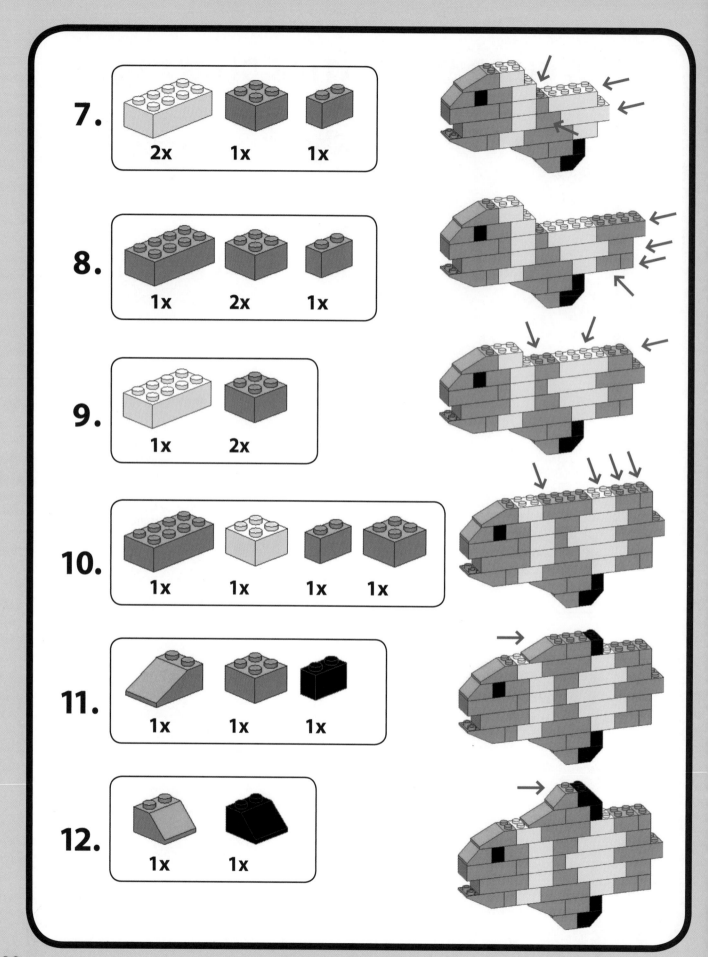

7. 2x 1x 1x

8. 1x 2x 1x

9. 1x 2x

10. 1x 1x 1x 1x

11. 1x 1x 1x

12. 1x 1x

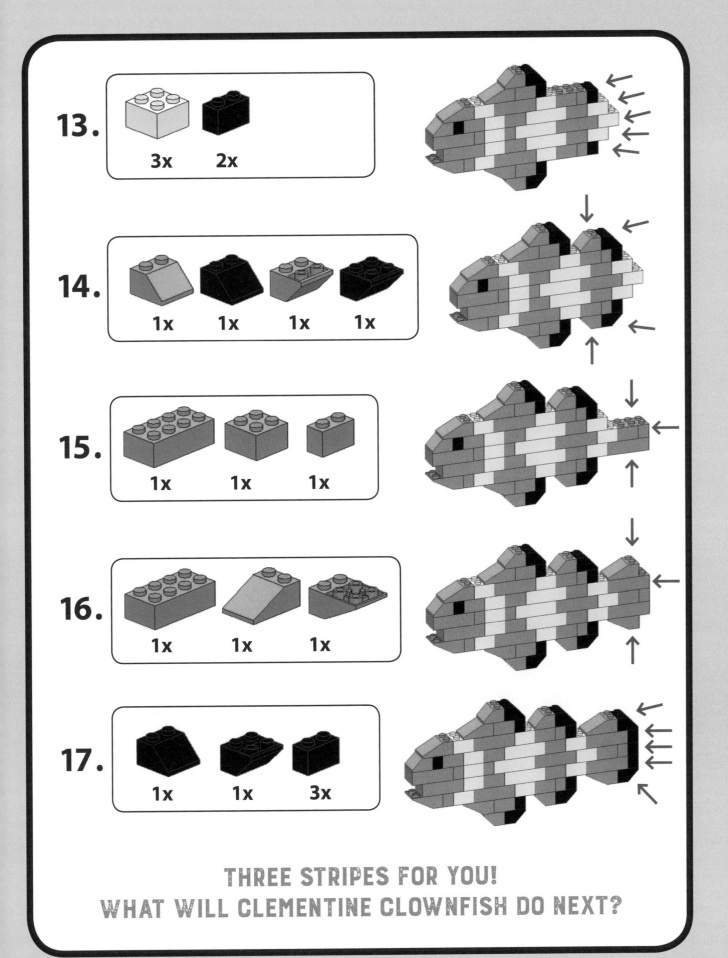

13. 3x 2x

14. 1x 1x 1x 1x

15. 1x 1x 1x

16. 1x 1x 1x

17. 1x 1x 3x

THREE STRIPES FOR YOU!
WHAT WILL CLEMENTINE CLOWNFISH DO NEXT?

WELCOME TO THE FARM!

REINA RABBIT

Level: EASY

LEARNING CONCEPTS

1. Recognize and name colors

2. Sort & group common objects by color, shape, and size

3. Count numbers, from 1 to 4

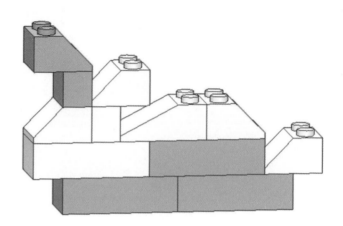

READY...GET SET...SORT!

GREY

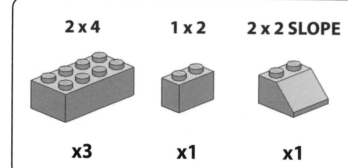

2 x 4	1 x 2	2 x 2 SLOPE
x3	x1	x1

WHITE

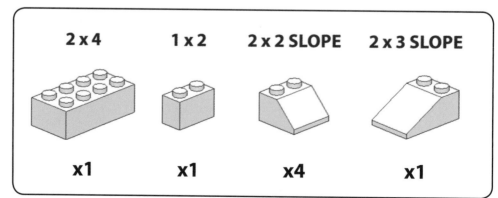

2 x 4	1 x 2	2 x 2 SLOPE	2 x 3 SLOPE
x1	x1	x4	x1

LET'S BUILD REINA RABBIT!

1.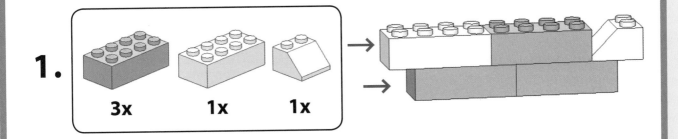

3x 1x 1x

2.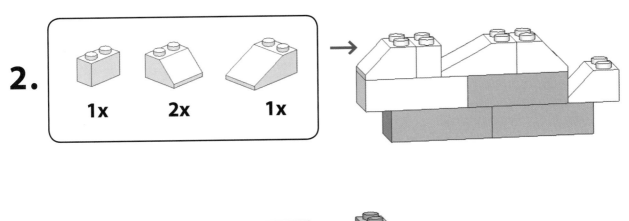

1x 2x 1x

3.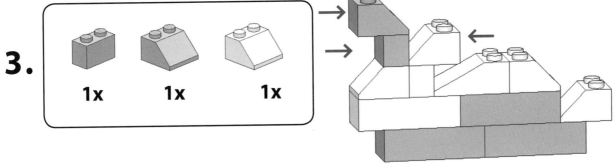

1x 1x 1x

HOP-PITI-DOO! GREAT JOB!
REINA RABBIT IS LOOKING FOR A CARROT.
WHERE SHOULD SHE LOOK?

SAMMY SHEEP

Level: EASY

LEARNING CONCEPTS

1. Recognize and name colors

2. Sort & group common objects by color, shape, and size

3. Count numbers, from 1 to 4

READY...GET SET...SORT!

BLACK

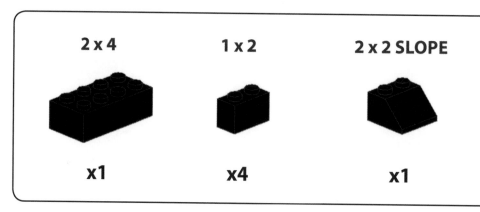

2 x 4	1 x 2	2 x 2 SLOPE
x1	x4	x1

WHITE

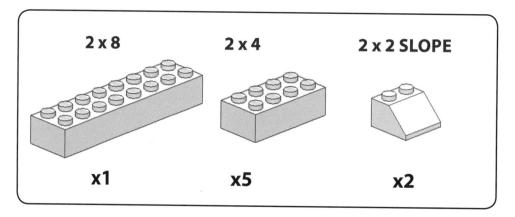

2 x 8	2 x 4	2 x 2 SLOPE
x1	x5	x2

LET'S BUILD SAMMY SHEEP!

1. 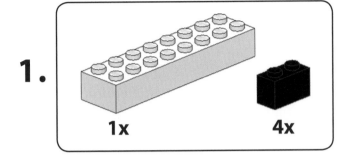 1x 4x

2. 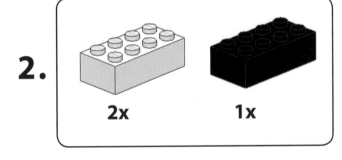 2x 1x

3. 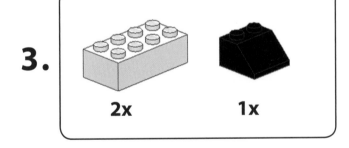 2x 1x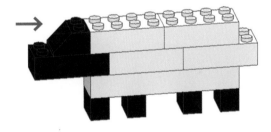

4. 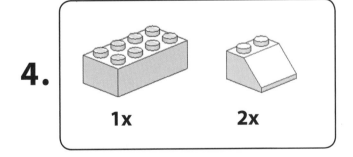 1x 2x

BAA-BAA-BEAUTIFUL BUILD!
HOW DOES SAMMY SHEEP'S WOOL FEEL?

PETER PIG

Level: EASY

LEARNING CONCEPTS

1. Sort & group common objects by color, shape, and size

2. Recognize written numerals range 1 to 10 and count objects up to 10

3. Follow top-to-bottom, left-to-right direction sequences

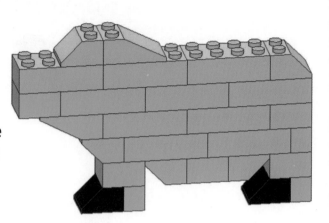

READY...GET SET...SORT!

PINK

2 x 4	2 x 2	1 x 2
x10	x5	x3

2 x 2 SLOPE	2 x 3 SLOPE	2 x 2 SLOPE INVERTED	3 x 2 SLOPE INVERTED
x2	x1	x3	x1

BLACK

2 x 2 SLOPE

x2

LET'S BUILD PETER PIG!

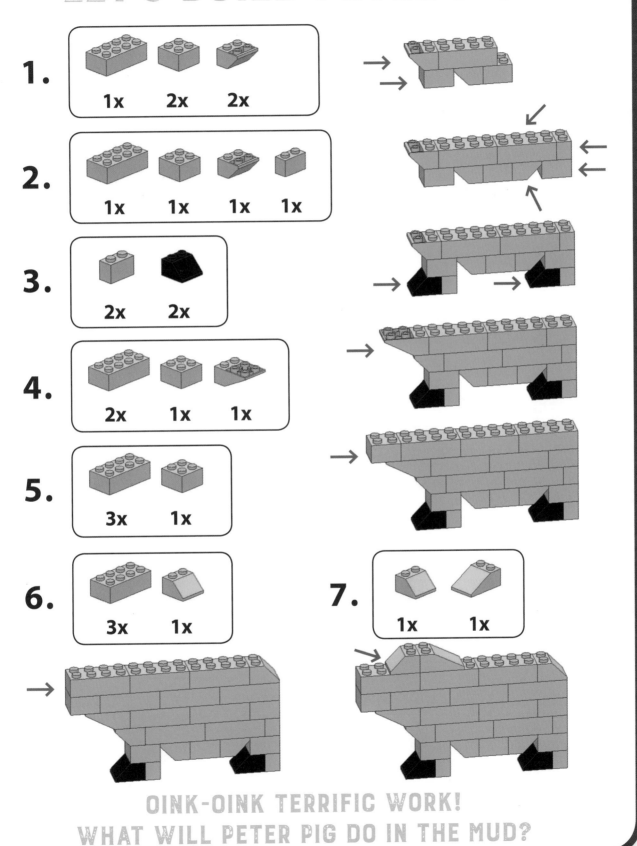

1. 1x 2x 2x

2. 1x 1x 1x 1x

3. 2x 2x

4. 2x 1x 1x

5. 3x 1x

6. 3x 1x

7. 1x 1x

OINK-OINK TERRIFIC WORK!
WHAT WILL PETER PIG DO IN THE MUD?

CHICKY CHICKEN

Level: EASY

LEARNING CONCEPTS

1. Sort & group common objects by color, shape, and size

2. Recognize written numberals range 1 to 6 and count objects up to 6

3. Follow left-to-right direction sequence

READY...GET SET...SORT!

ORANGE

2 x 3 SLOPE	3 x 2 SLOPE INVERTED
x1	x1

RED

2 x 4	2 x 2 SLOPE	2 x 3 SLOPE
x3	x4	x2

YELLOW

2 x 4	2 x 2	1 x 2	2 x 2 SLOPE	2 x 2 SLOPE INVERTED
x6	x5	x2	x1	x4

LET'S BUILD CHICKY CHICKEN!

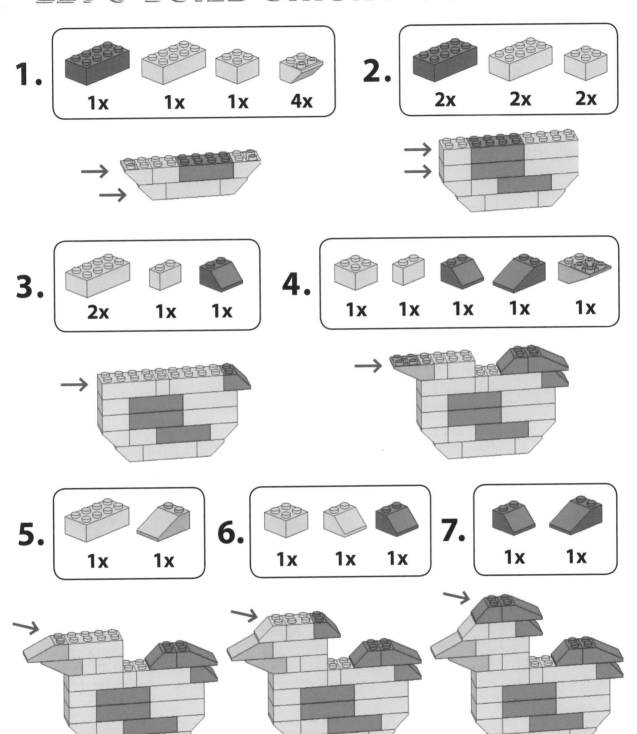

1. 1x 1x 1x 4x

2. 2x 2x 2x

3. 2x 1x 1x

4. 1x 1x 1x 1x 1x

5. 1x 1x

6. 1x 1x 1x

7. 1x 1x

COCK-A-DOODLE-DOO! HOW MANY EGGS DOES
CHICKY CHICKEN HAVE IN HER NEST?

HENRY HORSE

Level: MEDIUM

LEARNING CONCEPTS

1. Sort & group common objects by color, shape, and size

2. Recognize written numerals range 1 to 8 and count objects up to 8

3. Follow top-to-bottom direction sequence

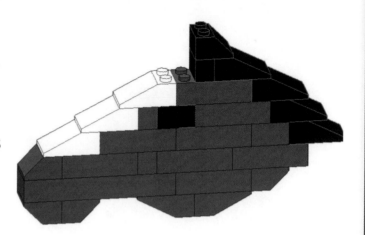

READY...GET SET...SORT!

BROWN

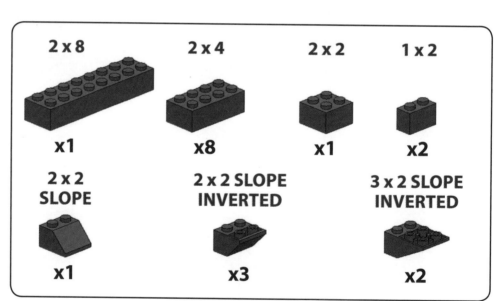

2 x 8	2 x 4	2 x 2	1 x 2
x1	x8	x1	x2

2 x 2 SLOPE	2 x 2 SLOPE INVERTED	3 x 2 SLOPE INVERTED
x1	x3	x2

BLACK

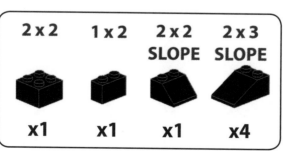

2 x 2	1 x 2	2 x 2 SLOPE	2 x 3 SLOPE
x1	x1	x1	x4

WHITE

2 x 3 SLOPE
x3

LET'S BUILD HENRY HORSE!

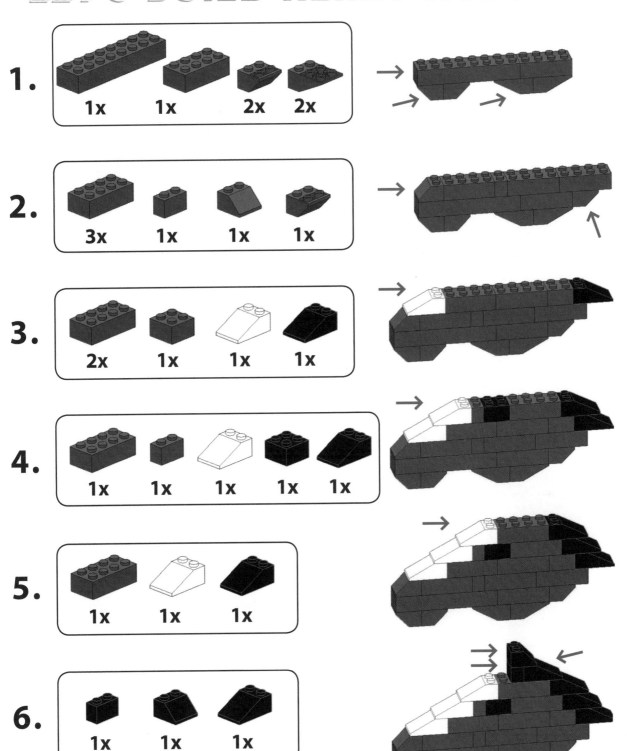

1. 1x 1x 2x 2x

2. 3x 1x 1x 1x

3. 2x 1x 1x 1x

4. 1x 1x 1x 1x 1x

5. 1x 1x 1x

6. 1x 1x 1x

NEEIIGGGHHH-TASTIC! HENRY HORSE
WANTS TO GO FOR A RIDE. WHERE SHOULD HE GO?

WINKY WOLF

Level: MEDIUM

LEARNING CONCEPTS

1. Sort & group common objects by color, shape, and size

2. Recognize written numerals range 1 to 5 and count objects up to 5

3. Follow top-to-bottom, left-to-right direction sequences

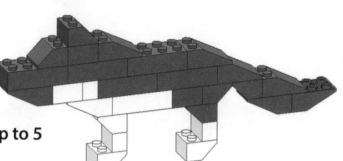

READY...GET SET...SORT!

DARK GREY

2 x 4	2 x 2	2 x 2 SLOPE
x5	x2	x2
2 x 3 SLOPE	2 x 2 SLOPE INVERTED	3 x 2 SLOPE INVERTED
x4	x3	x3

WHITE

2 x 4	2 x 2	1 x 2	2 x 2 SLOPE INVERTED	3 x 2 SLOPE INVERTED
x1	x1	x3	x3	x1

LET'S BUILD WINKY WOLF!

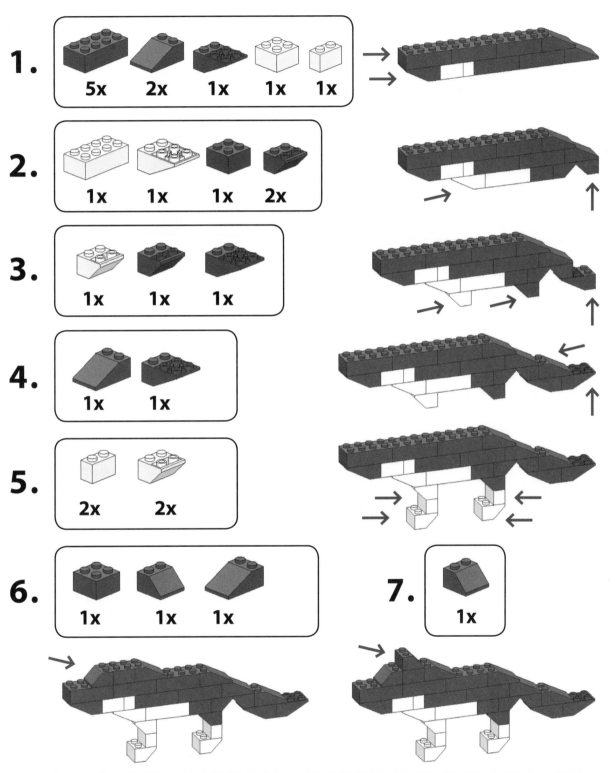

1. 5x 2x 1x 1x 1x

2. 1x 1x 1x 2x

3. 1x 1x 1x

4. 1x 1x

5. 2x 2x

6. 1x 1x 1x

7. 1x

YOU'RE SUPER-HOWLING! WINKY WOLF WANTS TO
SEE THE MOON; WHAT SHAPE DOES HE SEE?

Level: MEDIUM

LEARNING CONCEPTS

1. Sort & group common objects by color, shape, and size

2. Understand positioning concepts of "above," "under," and "beside"

3. Follow top-to-bottom, left-to-right direction sequences

READY...GET SET...SORT!

LIGHT BLUE

2 x 4	2 x 2	1 x 2
x3	x3	x6

2 x 2 SLOPE	2 x 2 SLOPE INVERTED	3 x 2 SLOPE INVERTED
x7	x4	x1

WHITE

2 x 4	2 x 2	1 x 2	2 x 2 SLOPE
x2	x3	x2	x4

2 x 3 SLOPE	2 x 2 SLOPE INVERTED	3 x 2 SLOPE INVERTED
x1	x3	x1

LET'S BUILD DANIEL DOG!

1.

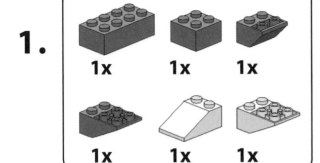

1x   1x   1x

1x   1x   1x

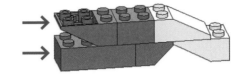

2.

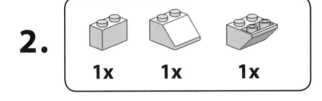

1x   1x   1x

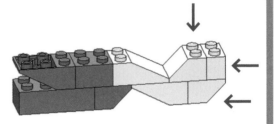

3.

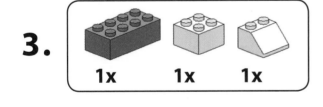

1x   1x   1x

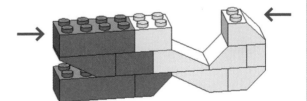

4.

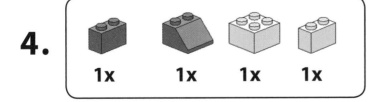

1x   1x   1x   1x

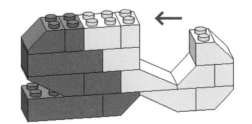

5.

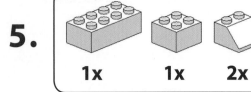 1x 1x 2x 1x

6.

1x 1x

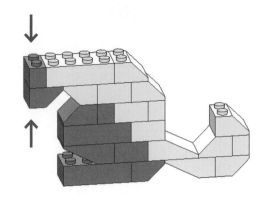

7.

3x 1x

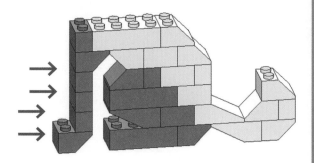

8.

1x 1x

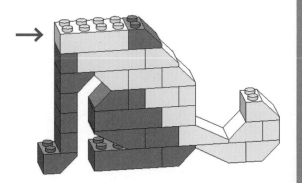

84

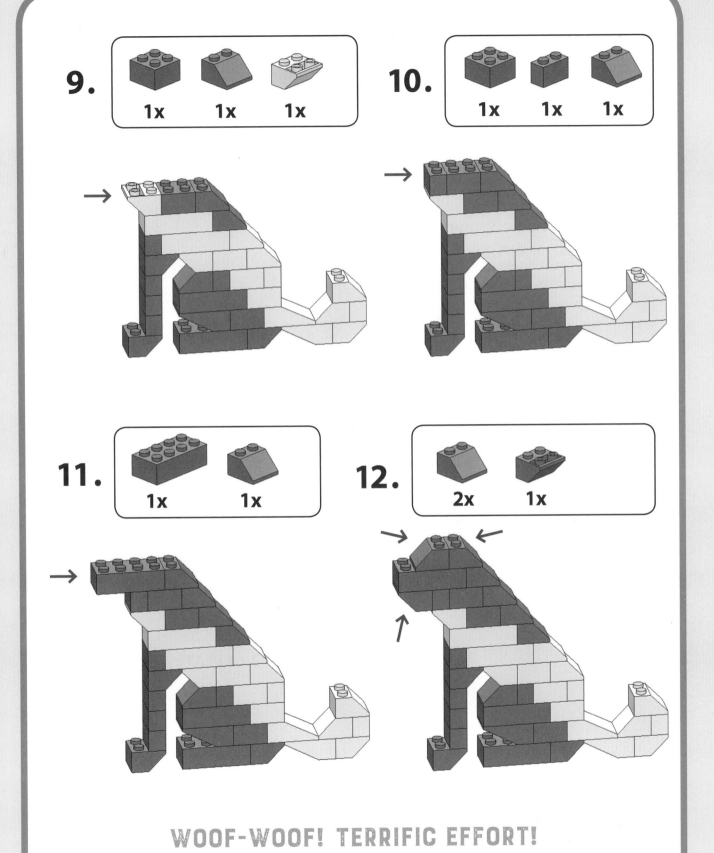

9. 1x 1x 1x

10. 1x 1x 1x

11. 1x 1x

12. 2x 1x

WOOF-WOOF! TERRIFIC EFFORT!
WHERE DID DANIEL DOG BURY HIS BONE?

GABBY GOOSE

Level: ADVANCED

LEARNING CONCEPTS

1. Sort & group common objects by color, shape, and size

2. Understand positioning concepts of "above," "under," and "beside"

3. Follow left-to-right direction sequence

READY...GET SET...SORT!

YELLOW

2 x 2	1 x 2	2 x 4 PLATE	1 x 2 PLATE
x1	x1	x2	x1

2 x 2 SLOPE	2 x 3 SLOPE	2 x 2 SLOPE INVERTED
x1	x1	x1

WHITE

2 x 4	2 x 2	1 x 2	2 x 4 PLATE	1 x 2 PLATE
x6	x7	x5	x1	x1

2 x 2 SLOPE	2 x 3 SLOPE	2 x 2 SLOPE INVERTED	3 x 2 SLOPE INVERTED
x5	x4	x6	x2

LET'S BUILD GABBY GOOSE!

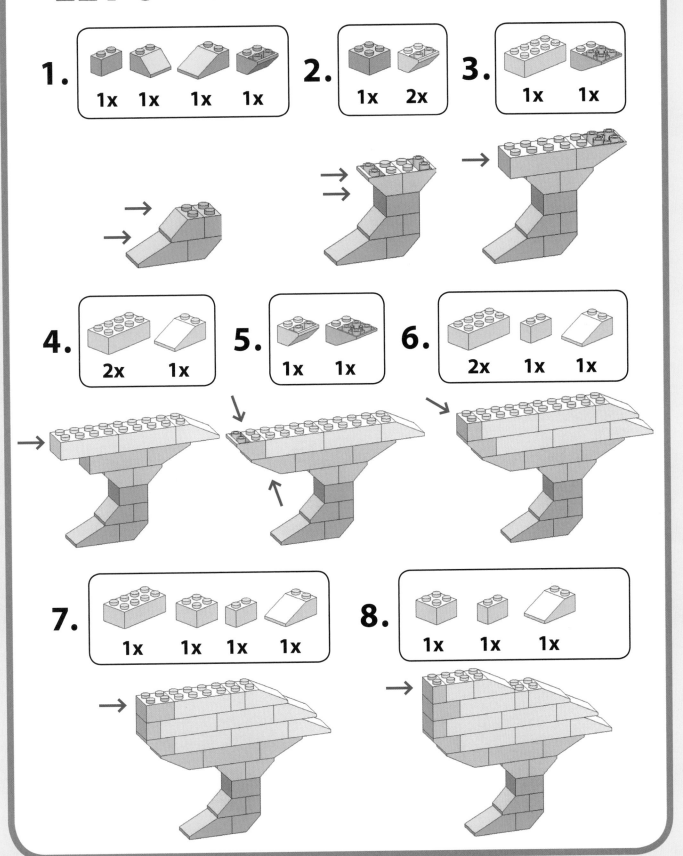

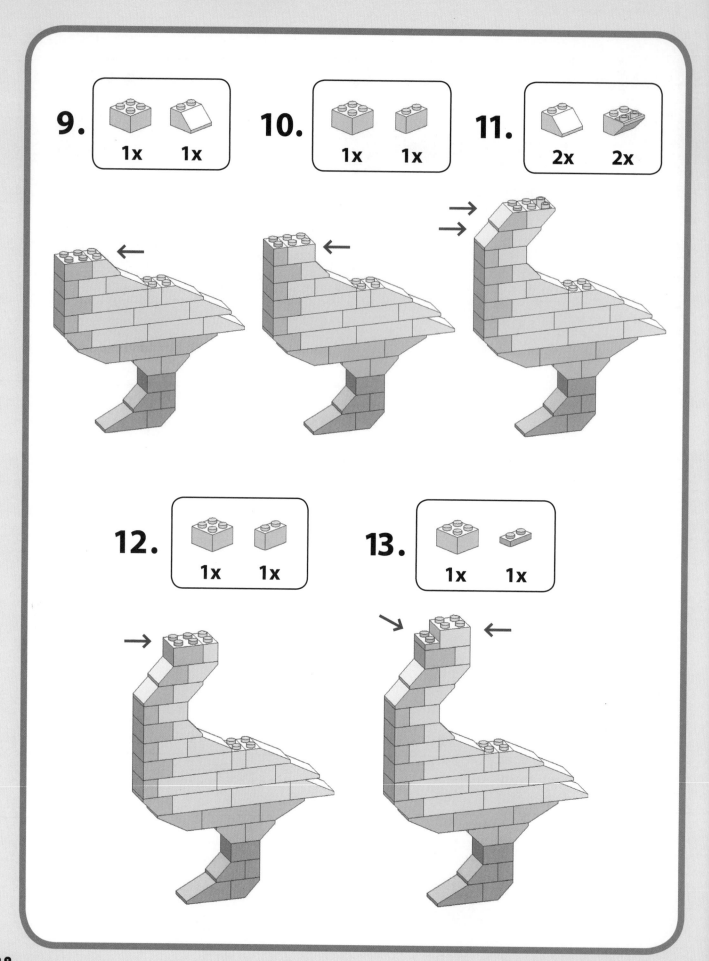

9. 1x 1x

10. 1x 1x

11. 2x 2x

12. 1x 1x

13. 1x 1x

14.

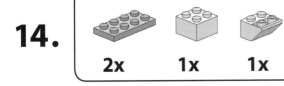

2x 1x 1x

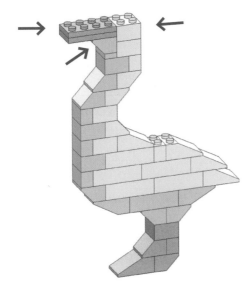

15.

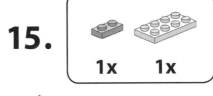

1x 1x

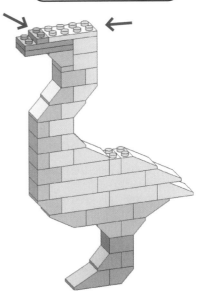

16.

2x

HONK HONK FOR
YOU! GABBY
GOOSE IS LOOKING
FOR FRIENDS. WHO
WILL SHE FIND?

DALLIA DUCK

Level: ADVANCED

LEARNING CONCEPTS

1. Sort & group common objects by color, shape, and size

2. Recognize different spatial relations using plate bricks

3. Follow top-to-bottom, left-to-right direction sequences

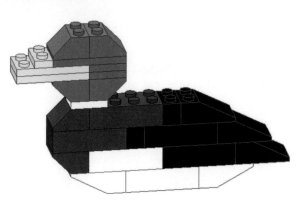

READY...GET SET...SORT!

WHITE

2 x 4	3 x 2 SLOPE INVERTED	2 x 2 PLATE
x2	x2	x1

BLACK

2 x 4	1 x 2	2 x 3 SLOPE
x2	x2	x3

GREEN

2 x 2 SLOPE	2 x 2 SLOPE INVERTED	2 x 4 PLATE	2 x 2 PLATE
x2	x2	x1	x2

BROWN

2 x 4	2 x 2 SLOPE	2 x 2 SLOPE INVERTED
x2	x1	x1

YELLOW

2 x 4 PLATE	1x2 PLATE
x2	x1

LET'S BUILD DALLIA DUCK!

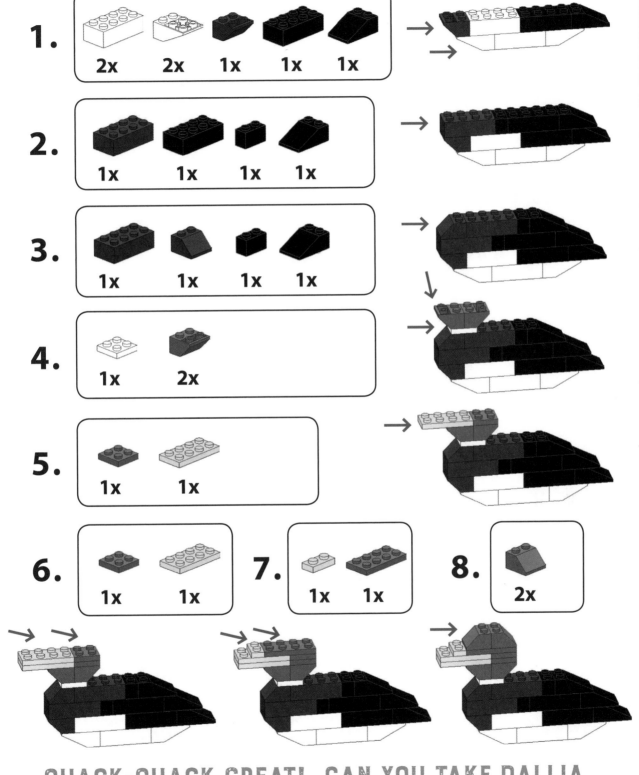

QUACK-QUACK GREAT! CAN YOU TAKE DALLIA DUCK FOR A SWIM IN THE POND?

RALLY RAM

Level: ADVANCED

LEARNING CONCEPTS

1. Sort & group common objects by color, shape, and size

2. Follow positioning concepts of "above," "under," and "beside"

3. Follow top-to-bottom, left-to-right direction sequences

READY...GET SET...SORT!

GREY

2 x 2 SLOPE	2 x 2 SLOPE INVERTED	3 x 2 SLOPE INVERTED
x1	x5	x1

TAN

2 x 4	2 x 2	2 x 2 SLOPE INVERTED	3 x 2 SLOPE INVERTED
x1	x1	x3	x1

WHITE

2 x 8	2 x 2	2 x 4	1 x 2	2 x 2 SLOPE	2 x 3 SLOPE	2 x 2 SLOPE INVERTED	3 x 2 SLOPE INVERTED
x1	x1	x4	x2	x2	x4	x1	x1

BROWN

1 x 2	2 x 2 SLOPE	2 x 3 SLOPE
x1	x1	x3

BLACK

2 x 2 SLOPE INVERTED	2 x 2 ROUND
x2	x1

LET'S BUILD RALLY RAM!

1.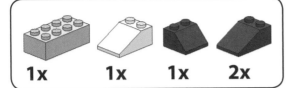

1x   1x   1x   2x

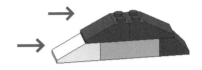

2.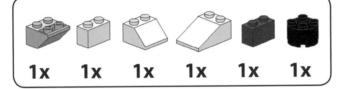

1x   1x   1x   1x   1x   1x

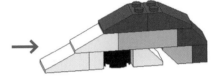

3.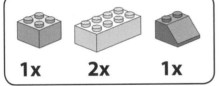

1x   2x   1x

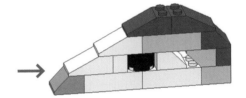

4.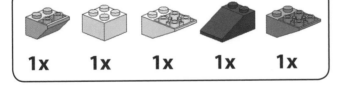

1x   1x   1x   1x   1x

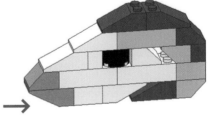

5.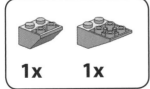

1x   1x

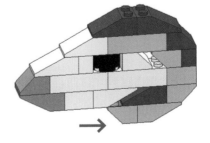

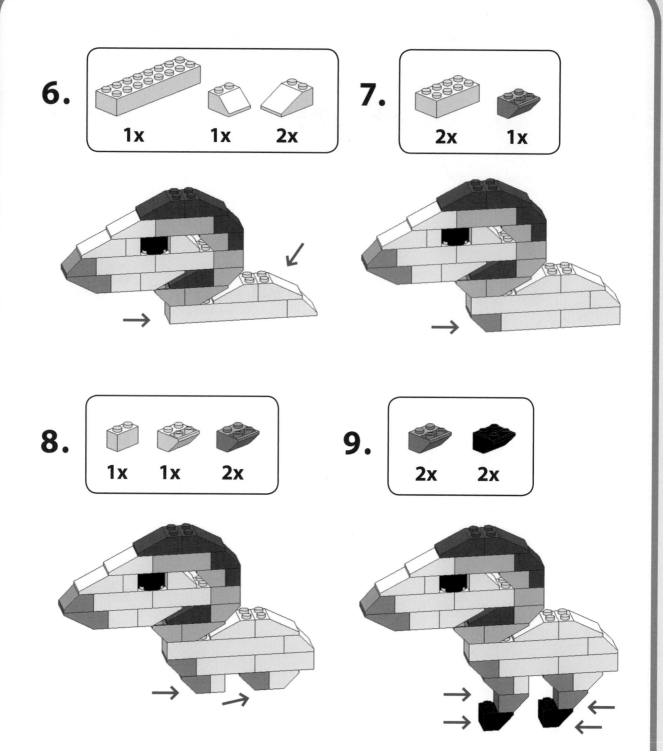

6. 1x 1x 2x

7. 2x 1x

8. 1x 1x 2x

9. 2x 2x

TWO HORNS UP! RALLY RAM LIKES TO CLIMB. WHERE WILL HE GO?

ABOUT THE AUTHORS

DESIGNER PAUL BACIO and editorial reviewer Elaine Bacio have three kids—Caleb, Joy, and Abby—who absolutely *love* brick-building. Paul, a former youth pastor and brick-building summer camp curriculum developer, is always inspiring his children and students to branch out into building imaginative new sets and ideas. Elaine is a certified health coach and a homeschooling mom. The couple live with their children in San Mateo, California.

CO-DESIGNER SOFIA CHEN is a fourth grader at Hugo Reid Elementary School. Sofia loves playing brick-building with Natalie, her little sister, after school—every day. Besides playing with bricks, Sofia also enjoys drawing, playing the piano and the viola, gardening, and helping her mom fundraise money for special-needs children. She lives with her parents, project editor Ann Kositchotitana and her husband, Ronald Chen, and her little sister, Natalie, in Arcadia, California.